Reclaiming Self

Issues and Resources
for Women Abused by Intimate Partners

edited by Leslie M. Tutty and Carolyn Goard

Third in the Hurting and Healing Series on Intimate Violence
Co-published by Fernwood Publishing
and RESOLVE (Research and Education for Solutions to Violence and Abuse)

Editing: Eileen Young
Cover art and design: Larissa Holman
Design and production: Beverley Rach
Printed and bound in Canada by: Hignell Printing Limited

A publication of:
Fernwood Publishing
Box 9409, Station A
Halifax, Nova Scotia
B3K 5S3
www.fernwoodbooks.ca
and
RESOLVE (Research and Education for Solutions to Violence and Abuse)
108 Isbister Building, University of Manitoba,
Winnipeg, Manitoba, R3T 2N2

Fernwood Publishing Company Limited gratefully acknowledges the financial support of the Department of Canadian Heritage and the Canada Council for the Arts for our publishing program.

Le Conseil des Arts | The Canada Council
du Canada | for the Arts

NOVA SCOTIA
Tourism and Culture

National Library of Canada Cataloguing in Publication Data

Main entry under title:

Reclaiming self: issues and resources for women abused by intimate partners

Includes bibliographical references.
ISBN 1-55266-077-X

1. Abused women—Canada. 2. Abused women—Services for—Canada.
I. Tutty, Leslie Maureen II. Goard, Carolyn

HV6626.23.C3R42 2002   362.82'92'0971   C2002-900390-3

Contents

4

Foreword

Ann Cameron

This "slim volume," *Reclaiming Self*, addresses critical issues in woman abuse, affording a broad perspective on this challenging social issue. Both theory and intervention frontiers will be advanced by the knowledge disseminated here. Those committed to alleviate and ultimately eliminate intimate battery will greet this book with enthusiasm, because we know that if we work closely with women themselves, with their support networks, with those who have previously been marginalized, and with topics previously ignored, our work will be more richly informed and more deeply grounded.

This volume, subtitled *Issues and Resources for Women Abused by Intimate Partners*, is one of many fine outcomes of the work of the prairie Research and Education for Solutions to Violence and Abuse (RESOLVE) Research Centre. It brings together community and academe; it reflects the work of a range of disciplines; it addresses the situations of all manner of participants, and especially some who have been traditionally excluded from our view. So let me highlight some of the valuable lessons I believe this RESOLVE collaboration on woman abuse will teach us.

First, Jane Ursel maps traditional criminal justice responses onto the transitional process many women experience in escaping intimate abuse, giving poignant evidence of the need for special family courts attuned to critical protection issues. Women in the long process of leaving an abusive situation need solutions very different from the single-incident mentality of traditional legal responses. Not only does a family court need to be configured to support those it serves, but legal professionals also need a deeper understanding of woman abuse and its ramifications, if it is to serve all vulnerable family members adequately.

Leslie Tutty and Michael Rothery, in evaluating the impacts of shelter experiences on women in transition, describe women's challenging paths subsequent to their experiences in transition shelters. This study attests to the pivotal long-term impacts of shelters on the women they serve and maybe even save.

Janice Ristock opens the door to an understanding regarding certain critical issues in same-sex intimate abuse. Specifically, lesbian partner-abuse often plays out before a backdrop of denial, invisibility and social exclusion, not to mention the pernicious interlocking systems of privilege and oppression. Interviews were conducted with women in six Canadian cities, and a full book is in the making. This is a topic that heretofore had not been on the agenda of most woman-abuse researchers.

Kendra Nixon shows that child protection workers, in their haste to help children living in abusive circumstances, may not appreciate the devastation to children of workers' insensitivity to the plight of their mothers. She reports the risks women and their families encounter in the face of the lack of training of child protection workers in identifying what is in the best interest of the child. A mother does not need to be told, "Either leave your partner, or lose your children." This chapter offers suggestions for better practices and for better professional (in this instance, child protection) training. Nixon says: "In situations of woman abuse, good child protection also includes good protection of mothers."

Jeannette Moldon reveals the healing grace of group therapy that gives women in transition efficacious voice in their recovery by affirming their life narratives. The group process in the validation of narratives of women recovering from abuse from an intimate partner is a significant segment of the story of how one moves on with integrity and self-respect.

This book calls for improvement in the practices of many helping professionals. It is set in the Canadian context; it addresses issues in our own backyard; and yet it will have universal interest to, and ultimately be required reading for, all those concerned about reducing and preventing the devastation which intimate abuse brings to the lives of women and children. Each unique piece of this patchwork sampler of research, much of which was conducted through RESOLVE, gives recognition to the fact that woman abuse is a multiply determined challenge in our culture and that victory over it will only emerge with a "whole village" of solutions.

Acknowledgements

This collaboration was made possible because of the commitment of RESOLVE (Research and Education for Solutions to Violence and Abuse) to present and disseminate research results that suggest how to intervene more effectively and prevent violence and abuse. We thank RESOLVE for supporting this project, in particular Jane Ursel, director of the RESOLVE Network, and Caroline Piotrowski, chair of the publication committee.

The research presented in this volume represents collaborations between academics, community agencies and women affected by intimate partner violence. Each group made a unique contribution. The academics and graduate students (at the time of the study) provided research expertise and considerable time both in conducting the research and writing the chapters. The service agencies and government systems gave access to their centres, service providers and the women with whom they work. Finally, and of great importance, women gave voice to their experiences, lifting the veil of secrecy from the private domain which they shared with violent partners.

Many individuals assisted in bringing this book to publication. Dr. Ann Cameron and an anonymous reviewer read the entire volume and gave invaluable feedback. Their thoughtful comments greatly assisted the chapter authors and editors in revising early drafts to ensure that our points were clearly made. We also thank Ann for writing the foreword to this volume at a time when she was especially busy and had already been more than generous in donating her time to RESOLVE Alberta. Carolyn and I are especially grateful to Wayne Anthony of Fernwood Publishing for his guidance and patience throughout the process. He is a wonderful editor and has a sharp eye for the essence of arguments and debates. Thanks also to Eileen Young for editing the final manuscript and to Beverley Rach for design and production.

About the Contributors

Carolyn Goard, M.A., has worked as a chartered psychologist in Alberta since 1973. Her positions include eight years as a clinician in a children's hospital; twenty-one years as a clinician and program manager at Calgary Family Services and five years in private practice. Currently, Carolyn is the Co-Director of the YWCA Family Violence Prevention Centre and Sheriff King Home in Calgary, an agency that serves women, men and children who have witnessed, and/or perpetrated abusive behaviour in an intimate relationship.

Jeannette Moldon holds a Masters Degree in clinical social work from the University of Calgary. She resides in Lethbridge, Alberta, and is a private practice therapist specializing in working with women who have experienced abuse and trauma.

Kendra Nixon is the Community Research Development Coordinator for RESOLVE Alberta. Kendra has worked as both a counsellor and advocate for battered women and a child protection worker in Ontario. She recently completed her Master of Social Work degree. Her thesis research explored child welfare policy and woman abuse.

Janice L. Ristock, Ph.D., is a professor of Women's Studies at the University of Manitoba. Recent publications include *No More Secrets: Violence in Lesbian Relationships* (2002, New York: Routledge) and *Inside the Academy and Out: Lesbian/Gay/Queer Studies and Social Action* (co-edited with Catherine Taylor, 1998, University of Toronto Press). Janice's current work includes examining the effects of a legislative reform in Australia that extends the *Domestic Violence Act* to include same-sex relationships but offers no additional resources (funding or training) to service organizations affected by this change.

Michael Rothery, Ph.D., is a professor with the University of Calgary's Faculty of Social Work. His research and writing focus on social work services to families, with a special interest in family violence.

Leslie Tutty, Ph.D., is a professor with the Faculty of Social Work at the University of Calgary where she teaches courses in both clinical social work methods and research. Her research focus over the past fifteen years has been violence prevention and treatment for those affected by intimate partner violence. She has served as the Academic Research Co-ordinator of RESOLVE Alberta since 1999.

Jane Ursel, Ph.D., is an associate professor in the Department of Sociology at the University of Manitoba and Director of RESOLVE, a tri-provincial network on research and education for solutions to violence and abuse. She is the director of a longitudinal study of the Winnipeg Family Violence Court and is involved in social policy analysis and development.

Chapter One

Woman Abuse in Canada
An Overview
Leslie M. Tutty and Carolyn Goard

The discovery of the extent and the serious nature of the abuse of women by their intimate partners took most of North American society by surprise. Before the early 1970s, the public knew little of the problem of "wife battering," as it was then called. It seemed inconceivable that husbands would strike their wives, let alone beat and severely injure them. Such behaviour must surely be rare and represent outmoded, nineteenth-century beliefs about women being essentially the property of their husbands.

Of course, woman abuse has always existed. Evan Stark (1984) noted that during the past century concern about women being battered by their husbands has resurfaced into public awareness in cycles of approximately twenty years, only to fade again into obscurity. The most recent identification of woman abuse, by the grassroots women's movement in the 1960s, led to the re-emergence of the problem from the privacy of the home to the public arena, as emergency shelters developed across North America. Shelters became important because traditional services, including medical, child welfare, mental health, police and judicial services, were not providing the necessary help for battered women (Davis, Hagen, and Early, 1994; Johnson, Crowley, and Sigler, 1992); this is still often the case. Yet even today, with national incidence studies, such as one recently conducted by Statistics Canada (2000) highlighting the continuation of the problem, there are those who debate the seriousness of the issue and the need to fund services for abused women.

There is considerable Canadian and American research on women abused by their intimate partners. There is also much debate and controversy over why it happens and why families stay together when life inside these homes is so traumatic. What we know less about is

how best to help women and their children to prevent both the imme-
diate and long-term serious consequences of being abused. Various
systems, such as the shelter, child welfare and justice systems, have
adapted their procedures or developed new ones to this end; but can
they adequately respond to such complex issues? The major focus of
this book is an examination of how well such interventions work.

Before we examine some of what we know about women abused
by their intimate partners, we'd like to introduce you to two women
whose partners were abusive and who sought safety in an emergency
shelter for abused women. The women were interviewed for the study
presented in Chapter Two.

> Brianne is thirty-three years of age. She was born and brought
> up in a close family in Ontario. She completed high school but
> had no further education or job training. After graduation, she
> worked in a number of low-paid retail jobs. Although Brianne
> had known Greg since high school, they hadn't formed a cou-
> ple relationship until about ten years ago when he came back
> to their hometown after having served a five-year prison term
> for armed robbery. As a child, Greg was not a good student and
> had dropped out of school in Grade 8. He came from a large
> family and both his parents abused alcohol. As a teen, Greg fell
> in with a rowdy group of friends and supported himself through
> selling drugs and breaking and entering homes.
>
> Greg and Brianne met one night in a bar and connected
> immediately. One of the reasons that they remained a couple
> was Brianne's compassion for Greg's unhappy family life and
> experiences. In the interview she commented, "He has a drink-
> ing problem, he has a drug problem and he has a problem
> because he's been in jail for so long. He's had a lot of bad luck.
> I used to look at him and think, 'poor human being ... how
> could anyone do that?' When you're in jail, there's a lot of bad
> things that can happen and almost everything did."
>
> Although they never actually lived together, they had
> three children, currently aged from two to eight years. Brianne
> went on social assistance after her first child was born because,
> with young children, it was very difficult to find work that
> could support them all. Greg began abusing Brianne soon after
> they got together. As Brianne noted, "It could be because I got
> pregnant right away. He went progressively, but really fast. It
> started where he would punish himself by punching brick
> walls on the outside, or playing a game where he wouldn't
> come in. He'd stay on my porch all night. It'd be rainy and cold
> but he wouldn't come in. And it didn't take long until it got

worse. He didn't like my friends and that got uncomfortable. All of a sudden I was alone. Then he started yelling and throwing things."

Although Brianne tried repeatedly to end the relationship, Greg threatened to sue her for custody of the children. "I hated being scared that he would take my little kids away from me. The incident that hurt my feelings the most was when I was pregnant with my last baby. It was the beginning and he came in here, threw me down and tried to put me through the patio doors. He was kicking me in the back, he had my hair, and he was going to punch me. The baby was not even a year old and the other kids were screaming and running all over the place. He pushed me toward them and into the highchair ... our baby was in the highchair. That was the worst beating that I got, but that was not the scariest time. The scariest time was when I thought he was going to shoot me." After the latter incident, Brianne took her children and entered a local emergency shelter for abused women.

Brianne's story perhaps reflects our stereotypes of abused women and their partners. The women are receiving welfare, the men are unemployed, criminals, and generally violent. Greg was under the influence of alcohol and drugs every time that he abused Brianne. As a contrast, let's look at Sheryl's experience.

Sheryl, now aged twenty-eight, grew up in Alberta in a rural neighbourhood. Her parents were farmers and had financial problems but were not abusive. Sheryl completed high school and spent several years in college majoring in criminology. She met her first husband while a student and, after becoming pregnant with one child, was a stay-at-home mother. The marriage broke up fairly amicably a year or so later. Sheryl met her current husband, Corey, at a church fund-raiser. Corey had completed high school but had no post-secondary education. He had a steady full-time job as an auto-mechanic. They married and quickly had two more children.

About a month after marrying, Corey began criticizing Sheryl. The worst incident of physical abuse was when "I was pregnant with our second child, and he beat me quite badly ... there had been some random acts before but never as violent as that."

Sheryl insisted that Corey seek help or she would leave. He went to counselling and, although the physical violence stopped, the emotional and verbal abuse did not. However, the relationship remained relatively stable until, as Sheryl describes, "My husband sexually assaulted me three months ago and we've been separated since then. He raped me because he believed I had been with another man. Corey had always been so respectful of me sexually; I would have never in a million years believed that this could have happened. So, emotionally, it was extremely shocking." Sheryl asked Corey to move out, but he returned about a month later: "Because I didn't go to the police and I didn't get a restraining order, and we're not legally divorced yet, there was nothing they could do to stop him." To keep her and her children safe, Sheryl went to a local women's emergency shelter.

Sheryl and Corey lived more middle-class lives than Brianne and Greg. Corey had a steady job, they regularly attended church, and Sheryl was home-schooling her three children. When Corey went for counselling after having perpetrated the one serious physically abusive incident early in their relationship, Sheryl believed that he would never again physically hurt her.

We have presented the narratives of Brianne and Sheryl to put a human face on the statistics about intimate partner violence. We'll return to their stories in the final chapter to see how they and their children fared after their shelter stay. The following section presents information and research about the extent and nature of woman abuse in Canada and how we explain the occurrence of such violence.

Woman Abuse by Intimate Partners: The Canadian Context

The seriousness of woman abuse, and the cost, not only to the women, but to their children as well, has become recognized over the past twenty years. How commonly it occurs has been a question of much debate. The prevalence of abuse against women varies according to different surveys. For example, the 1999 General Social Survey on Victimization concluded the following:

> 7% of people who were married or living in a common-law relationship experienced some type of violence by a partner during the previous 5 years. The 5-year rate of violence was similar for women (8%) and men (7%). Overall, this amounts to approximately 690,000 women and 549,000 men who had a current or former partner in the past five years and reported experiencing at least one incident of violence. (Statistics Canada, 2000, p. 5)

In comparison, another national study, the 1993 Violence Against

Women Survey that focused solely on women, estimated that "three in ten women currently or previously married in Canada have experienced at least one incident of physical or sexual violence at the hands of a marital partner" (Rodgers, 1994, p. 1). Such differences in estimates of abuse occur because of the manner in which violence is defined, for example, whether it includes forms of abuse other than physical. Nevertheless, the conclusion that from 7 to 30 percent of Canadian women have experienced violence from intimate partners is sobering.

Men are also abused by women partners to a similar degree; many studies, such as the 1999 General Social Survey on Victimization (Statistics Canada, 2000), have described this phenomenon. Why, then, is this not also a focus for the book? "Husband abuse," as it was originally termed, remains a contentious issue for some because it has not received the same high-profile media coverage, nor have shelters or treatment groups for men victims proliferated in the same way as they have for women. Several men's advocacy groups have become quite vocal, claiming that men's pain is being ignored and questioning the extent to which family violence services are almost exclusively targeted to women and child victims and to the men who perpetrate abuse against women.

There has, admittedly, been relatively little research on the experiences and consequences for men abused by partners (Tutty, 1999a). However, as the 1999 General Social Survey on Victimization clarifies, abuse against women by male partners tends to be more serious:

> Women were more than twice as likely as men to report being beaten, five times more likely to report being choked, and almost twice as likely to report being threatened by or having a gun or knife used against them. Men were more likely than women to report being slapped (57% versus 40%), having something thrown at them (56% versus 44%) and being kicked, bit or hit (51% versus 33%). (Statistics Canada, 2000, p. 5)

Repeated abuse of women by men occurs more often: 65 percent of women, compared to 54 percent of men, were assaulted on more than one occasion; 26 percent of women, as compared to 13 percent of men, were victimized more than ten times. The results of the abuse more often led to injury for women: 40 percent of women, compared to 13 percent of men who had reported violence in the past five years, were injured. Women were five times more likely than men to require medical attention for these injuries. Perhaps most informative is the finding that women fear their partners' violence to a significantly greater extent, with 38 percent of women compared to 7 percent of men fearing for their lives (Statistics Canada, 2000). Since a central focus of this book is services for those who seek assistance for abuse by intimate partners, almost every chapter describes only women as victims.

Johnson, a sociologist, has attempted, in a useful way, to reconcile the argument about whether the abuse of men is a significant issue; he suggests that two different forms of couple violence exist, identified by two different types of research (1995). A number of community survey studies use the Conflict Tactics Scale (Straus, 1990), that looks at aggressive acts in a context of resolving marital conflicts. The relatively high numbers of both men and women who admit using violent acts against each other has been described as "common couple violence." This term does not imply that it is acceptable, but that it happens often. Johnson suggests that in these cases a feminist analysis is less relevant to the way that "conflict occasionally 'gets out of hand,' leading usually to 'minor' forms of violence, and more rarely escalating into serious, sometimes even life-threatening forms of violence" (p. 285). In reviewing the nature of the abuse in such studies, Johnson found little tendency for the violence to increase over time, citing that "94% of perpetrators of minor violence do not go on to severe violence" (p. 286). Things "get out of hand" on average about once every two months, and may be initiated by either the man or the women.

In contrast, Johnson notes that the research that describes the experiences of battered women, mostly from in-depth interviews with women who have sought safety in emergency shelters or whose husbands are in treatment for wife assault, portrays a different type of abuse. The violence is severe, with beatings occurring on average more than twice a week, and almost entirely initiated by the husbands. The women are often abused throughout the relationship, and the violence increases in frequency and severity over time. Johnson labels this dynamic "patriarchal terrorism," and suggests that it is a product of "patriarchal traditions of men's right to control their women ... and involves the use of not only violence, but economic subordination, threats, isolation and their control tactics" (p. 284). Marital rape is also commonly associated with such abuse.

Johnson's distinction between these two different forms of intimate-partner violence is important because it explains the radically different views of the two groups of researchers in a way that acknowledges each. The researchers are studying different phenomena with little overlap in the samples. For example, men who systematically terrorize women partners are not likely to participate in a survey on violence, and their partners would be fearful to do so. The focus of this book is on the second type of abuse, using a feminist analysis.

What Do Abused Women Experience?

The physical violence perpetrated by men on their intimate partners takes many forms and is often present throughout the relationship, although the severity may increase over the years. While the context of initial violent acts may be a couple disagreement, the core issues are control and jealousy. In general, as well, the force of the violence far outweighs the import of the precipitating issue. Women are not simply pushed, shoved or slapped: they are beaten or injured where they are most vulnerable. Women often identify their first pregnancy as the start of the violence. Their partner may direct his physical aggression at the baby in her belly or at other female parts such as her breasts or genitals.

These men not only physically assault their partners, but are severely emotionally abusive, from threatening murder, stalking and raping partners to threatening to kidnap or to take legal custody of their children. According to Sackett and Saunders' 1999 research, there are four significant types of psychological abuse: ridiculing of personal traits, criticizing behaviour, ignoring and jealous control. In interviews, the women considered their partner's ridicule to be the most severe form of abuse. In addition to having experienced more physical abuse, the women residing in shelters reported more ridicule of their personal characteristics and more jealous control than the abused women living in the community.

While the public tends to be generally aware of physical aggression and injury as a major result of woman assault, the acknowledgement that sexual aggression often co-exists with physical aggression has received considerably less attention. Even mental health professionals and shelter workers may not ask about the possibility of marital rape despite the fact that the assaults may be ongoing throughout the relationship. As such, the traumatic consequences may be even more significant than for victims of non-marital rape (Campbell and Soeken, 1999; Riggs, Kilpatrick and Resnick, 1992; Monson and Langhinrichsen-Rohling, 1998; Whatley, 1993).

Some abusive men stalk their partners (Coleman, 1997), typically, but not always, after the women have left the relationship. Studies have estimated the percentage of women victims of domestic violence who are stalked is as high as 50 percent (Mechanic, Weaver and Resick, 2000; Wright, Burgess, Laszlo, McCrary and Douglas, 1996). Furthermore, it is not unusual for abused women with children to receive threats or fear that their partner may kidnap (Liss and Stahly, 1993) or take custody or their children (Kurtz, 1996).

Finally, some men murder their partners. Women who are separated from their partners are generally at more risk of being murdered than when cohabiting. Wilson and Daly (1992) found that a higher incidence of common-law relationships, separation from a partner and belonging to an ethnic group, including being of Aboriginal origin, as well as greater age differences were associated with spousal homicide rates. In a review of Canadian statistics from the last twenty-two years (1978 to 1997), Fitzgerald (1999) noted that spouses were the victims in 18 percent of all solved homicides and 48 percent of family-related incidents. He also reported that "Over the two decades, three times more wives than husbands were killed by their spouse (1,485 women and 442 men)" (1999, p. 35).

In summary, the abuse that women endure from intimate male partners can take many forms and typically extends throughout the relationship. Physical abuse always involves a psychological component. One story that illustrates this dramatically is recounted by Stark (1984), who interviewed women in emergency rooms in hospitals. A woman who denied that she had been battered, explained that her husband got his way by holding a gun to her head. Because she had not actually been hit for a number of years, she did not see herself as having been "battered." Other women may similarly deny current physical abuse, not seeing that the serious nature of past violence has a direct impact on their responses. While emotional abuse can have serious long-term consequences on intimate partners, some women experience such sadistic, brutal assaults from their partners that escaping the relationship may, in fact, put them at greater risk than staying.

What Causes Intimate Partner Abuse?

As early as 1979, Gelles and Straus identified fifteen different theoretical views that purport to explain domestic violence in general and why women remain in abusive relationships in particular. The theories fall into three categories: individual, social-psychological and socio-cultural. Individual theories examine variables that focus on the intrapsychic, individual and psychopathology of each member of the couple. These perspectives include masochism on the part of the women and mental illness on the part of the partner, drug and alcohol dependency, and neurobiological explanations such as head-injuries. In general, none of these explanations has been shown to be generally applicable to partner abuse.

Social-psychological theories, including social learning theory, exchange theory, symbolic interaction and attribution theory, examine psychological characteristics in combination with variables in the social environment. So, for example, being exposed as children to marital violence between one's parents has been examined as a cause of intimate partner violence as adults. This theory, also known as the intergenerational transmission of abuse, is often used to predict that men and women with such childhood histories might well not only become victims or persecutors in their intimate relationships, but, after leaving their partners, may again become involved in an abusive relationship. Considerable research suggests that while this holds true for many men, it is not the case for women, who often had no childhood exposure to violence and, having left an abusive partner, develop new non-violent relationships (Tutty, 1999b).

The third category of theories, the socio-cultural, includes functional, subculture-of-violence, general systems, conflict and intrafamilial resource theory. This perspective suggests that "social structured inequality and cultural attitudes and norms about family relationships" (Gelles and Straus, 1979) explain the occurrence of family violence.

Feminist theory also provides a socio-cultural explanation for woman abuse and has been adopted by the majority of agencies that offer services to abused women (Pressman, 1989). From a feminist perspective, much of the abuse that men direct at their partners is an effort to control to whom they have access and what they can do. Johnson's concept of "patriarchal terrorism," mentioned previously, uses feminist theory. Such abuse is not about marital conflict or managing anger, but about men restricting and preventing women from leaving or forming attachments to other men. The feminist perspective has been central in the development of women's shelters, interventions for women victims of abuse and the majority of interventions for male perpetrators. As can be seen in Chapter Three, it has more recently become important in the criminal justice response to the assault of intimate partners.

A more in-depth discussion of these theoretical frameworks is beyond the scope of this chapter. They are listed to demonstrate the breadth and diversity of thought utilized in attempts to understand the abuse of women by their intimate partners. Considerable research has focused on the social learning concept of learned helplessness (Walker, 1984) and on feminist perspectives of traditional male and female roles (Straus, Gelles and Steinmetz, 1980). While substantial debate has centred on arguing the merits of one framework over another, it is likely that each of the frameworks has a viewpoint that is valid for at least some subset of abused women and their spouses. A number of the theoretical frameworks apply to each battered woman. For example, not only might a battered woman be married to an alcoholic with traditional male role values, who becomes aggressive when she talks about working outside the home, but he may also have come from a violent home where he was abused as a child by his parents. Further, the woman may have religious beliefs that "marriage vows are sacred," and her family may instruct her that it is her responsibility to make the marriage work, if not for her own sake, then for the sake of the children. She may also be aware that after an abusive episode her husband is remorseful and non-violent for several weeks. In this example, more than one perspective explains why women might be abused or might stay with abusive partners. Two authors, one from a general systems point of view (Giles-Sims, 1983) and another from an ecological framework (Carlson, 1984), have developed models that integrate different theories. This is a more fitting perspective of woman abuse, which likely has multiple causes. However, as noted earlier, feminist principles have been meaningfully adopted in the major interventions to assist women abused by intimate partners.

The Effects of Being Abused by an Intimate Partner

Much of the early study of intimate partner violence searched for characteristics of women abused by intimate partners, initially suggesting such common variables as a feeling of helplessness (Hilberman and Munson, 1978; Walker, 1978), traditional sex-role orientation, social isolation (Wetzel and Ross, 1983; Pressman, 1989) and low self-esteem (Hilberman and Munson, 1978; Hartik, 1982). However, in 1990, Hotaling and Sugarman concluded that "after 15 years of empirical research on wife assault, few risk markers have been found that identify women at risk to violence in close relationships ... it is evident that researchers should focus greater attention on the perpetrators, the dynamics of the relationship, and the social environment in which the relationship exists" (p.12). While it may not be useful to focus on victim characteristics to understand how women might end up in an assaultive relationship, such traits are more usefully perceived as the result of living in a violent relationship and may be the targets of interventions such as support groups (Tutty, Bidgood, and Rothery, 1996).

Coping with an abusive relationship creates considerable anxiety, especially if the threats and physical abuse continue over time. Such stresses not uncommonly result in women reacting with depression, panic attacks, suicidal ideation or substance abuse (Alexander and Muenzenmaier, 1998; Gondolf, 1998; Tutty, 1998). Each of these symptoms could suggest the need for psychiatric intervention, implying that the abused woman is mentally unbalanced, a position that ignores the context of her situation. Rather than looking at various symptoms in isolation, however, a number of authors have identified a cluster of symptoms that are similar to those experienced by other victims of violence such as rape, robbery and physical assault. The symptoms include "anxiety, fears, recurrent nightmares, sleep and eating disorders, numbed affect, flashbacks, hypervigilance and increased startle responses" (Houskamp and Foy, 1991, p. 368). Women with a number of these problems can be considered as experiencing Posttraumatic Stress Disorder (PTSD), a condition that was recently included in the DSM-IV (Ristock, 1995). The advantage of the PTSD perspective is that, by definition, these problems are seen as "normal responses to abnormal occurrences in the lives of these victims" (Gleason, 1993, p. 62).

Lenore Walker (1991) also argues for adopting the PTSD conceptualization of the response to long-term partner abuse. As she explains:

> PTSD stresses the abnormal nature of the stressor that causes the mental health symptoms, not individual pathology. Such a disorder theoretically can happen to anyone who is placed in a similar situation. This takes the onus of blame away from the individual woman, yet still lets psychotherapists work with her in finding her own way to heal and move on with her life. (p. 22)

Researchers have recently found that a high proportion of women seeking help for domestic abuse have clinical levels of PTSD (Houskamp and Foy, 1991; Astin, Lawrence and Foy, 1993; Vitanza, Vogel and Marshall, 1995; Saunders, 1994; Tutty and Rothery, 1999). Higher levels of PTSD symptoms have been associated with more severe abuse, greater threat and more forced sex (Astin, Ogland-Hand, Coleman and Foy, 1995; Hughes and Jones, 2000; Kemp, Green, Hovanitz and Rawlings, 1995).

There is room for caution in considering the utility of any psychiatric diagnoses however, even one that includes the context of the relationship. Abused women might be further stigmatized by any medical diagnosis. Further, Walker (1991) notes "it is important to remember that not all battered women develop PTSD and even when they do, they may not need more than a support group with others in similar situations" (p. 28). The central point is that women abused by intimate partners often experience numerous reactions such as anxiety and depression. Rather than seeing these as indicative of a psychiatric syndrome, counsellors and support staff need to remember the context within which these reactions developed—living day to day in fear of abuse.

Barriers to Leaving an Abusive Partner

Perhaps the most commonly raised question with respect to women who are abused by intimate partners is why do they stay? A second closely related question is why some women, having left an abusive relationship by, for example, going to an emergency shelter, subsequently return to their partners. Rhodes and McKenzie (1998), who surveyed three decades of research on this topic, suggest that the assumption underlying these questions is that abused women wish to be abused. As mentioned previously, some of the early research on characteristics of women abused by intimate partners focused on whether the women were masochistic.

Such speculation is discounted by studies that suggest a number of factors that mitigate against women leaving abusive partners. A recently published study by Dobash, Dobash, Cavanagh and Lewis (2000) found that two thirds of the abused participants had left their partners at least once, others more frequently and 25 percent more than five times. Chief among their reasons for staying were the well-being of the children, desire to give the relationship another try, partner's promises of change and a lack of money or access to shelter.

Many women remain in assaultive relationships for years. The question of how and when a woman makes the decision to leave has been the focus of much early research. One study found that the choice to leave for a shelter was made two weeks to several months after a critical abusive incident (Giles-Sims, 1983). This incident was not necessarily the most violent but was characterized by three themes: fear that the children would be hurt, resentment at the husband for letting the children see their mother beaten and exposure of the violent pattern to people outside the family. Moore (1979) identified the presence of a strong support group, the absence of children and an increase in severity and frequency of the beatings as being associated with leaving sooner. Gelles (1976) found the most predictive factor to be financial independence. Similarly, the authors of a study of Ontario women who used a non-residential advocacy clinic (Greaves, Heapy and Wylie, 1988) found no relationship between the frequency, severity or the duration of the abuse and the leaving. Across all of these studies, factors other than the severity of the abuse are implicated in the decision to finally leave.

Children Exposed to Marital Violence

Women leave battering relationships as much for the sake of their children as for themselves (Wilson, Baglioni, and Downing, 1989). As mentioned previously, Giles-Sims (1983) found that two critical reasons prompting a woman to leave were fear that the children might be hurt and concern that the children had witnessed the abuse. MacLeod's Canadian study (1987) concluded that the abuse of children by their father or father figure was a major reason that women sought admission to an emergency shelter.

Children are also a reason that some women return to abusive partner relationships. In Smillie's (1991) interviews with several women who returned to their husbands despite having maintained themselves independently in the community for over a year, the women reported difficulties both with the stresses of being a single parent and with the children's behaviour. In Tutty's 1993 research on a shelter follow-up program, women raised similar issues and also felt guilty about depriving their children of a father. They often felt pressured by their children's pleas to reunite the family.

While the staff of battered women's shelters have long been concerned about the children who accompany their mothers to interval houses, it is only recently that more general concern has been expressed about the effects on children of witnessing violence between their parents (Jaffe, Wolfe and Wilson, 1990; Moore, Peplar, Mae, and Kates, 1989; Moore, Peplar, Weinberg, Hammond, Waddell, and Weiser, 1990). Children who have witnessed violence between their parents are at high risk for developing behavioural problems including either aggression or withdrawal (Fantuzzo and Lindquist, 1989; Jaffe et al., 1990; Moore et al., 1989), especially if they have been abused themselves (Hughes, 1988). Recent research has also identified such reactions as being a result of trauma, similar to the PTSD conceptualization of women's stress. Clearly the consequences of woman abuse extend beyond the bounds of the couple relationship.

Overview of the Book

As can be seen by the previous, albeit limited research review, although woman abuse was an almost invisible problem before the 1970s, it has remained a concern for the past three decades and has generated considerable research and intervention strategies. Why, then, write yet another book on the problem?

First, a great deal of the published research on abused women comes from the United States. Although this by no means rules out its applicability to women abused in Canada, the social, health and justice systems in this country are considerably different from those of our American neighbours, and an analysis of the needs and concerns of women in this country requires an understanding of this Canadian context. One major goal of this book, then, is to present Canadian research conducted by Canadian academics. Second, new approaches and interventions with abused women in Canada, such as courts that specialize in domestic abuse and expanded shelter programs, have developed. Several of the chapters provide details about how well such innovations are working. Third, as we become more aware of the complexities of abuse in intimate partner relationships, new problems emerge, for example, not only is abuse gendered such that women are victims and men perpetrators, but women in lesbian relationships may also be abused. Children who are exposed to marital violence are also affected. How, then, should provincial child welfare legislation address the need to protect children from adverse reactions? Several chapters in the book address these problems.

Chapter Two presents information about the experiences of over

200 residents of two emergency shelters for abused women. The chapter describes their backgrounds as well as the concerns that they present to shelter staff. The women's own words are used to document their past abuse, current fears and hopes for the future and how they are faring four to six months after their shelter residence.

Chapter Three presents research collected in a five-year period since the introduction of Winnipeg's Domestic Violence Court about ten years ago. The criminalization of the response to intimate partner violence by mandating police to charge assault in couple relationships has been controversial. Abused women often feel caught between the demands of their partners and the demands of the justice system to testify. The research presented in this chapter explores these dilemmas and the impact of a model of the justice response that was developed to be more sensitive to the women's needs.

The negative effects of children being exposed to intimate partner violence between their parents has been brought to the attention of the general public in the last decade or so. Several provinces have child welfare legislation that can be used to intervene when necessary. Chapter Four presents research based on interviews with eight child welfare workers about how they have utilized the Alberta child protection legislation with cases under their jurisdiction. The results raise some difficult yet important questions about balancing the needs and safety of children without placing undue responsibility on mothers who themselves have little control over their abuser.

Support groups for intimate partner violence have been one of the key interventions with women, whether offered in shelters or in the community. Chapter Five presents qualitative research that documents the responses and views of women who have participated in such groups. The women describe the benefits and challenges of being in the groups and the impact on their personal journey to living abuse-free lives.

Chapter Six describes results from a large national study of interviews with lesbian women abused by their partners that provides ideas about the way that such abuse parallels and differs from man-to-woman abuse in heterosexual relationships. The results challenge our conceptions of gender as the central driving force behind violence in intimate relationships, as it forces us to consider that women, too, may use power and control in abusive ways in their partnerships with other women.

Finally, Chapter Seven summarizes the learnings gleaned from, and the interconnections among, the research studies presented in each chapter. We conclude by identifying current challenges and offering practical suggestions about more adequately addressing the needs and problems faced by abused women.

It is our hope that this volume will provide information that is both interesting and relevant to the general public, as well as research findings that will validate and expand the research agendas of other academics and students of social sciences. We hope it will contribute practical suggestions so that professionals can more effectively intervene with abused women and their families. We do this from a perspective, eloquently proposed by Gondolf and Fisher (1988), that abused women should not be considered helpless victims but survivors who have endured significant hardship from the one person they believed they could trust the most—their intimate partner. We recognize that as women, we too could be trapped in similar circumstances, facing a multitude of very difficult choices including whether to leave and wrest children from their fathers, thereby becoming single mothers on often significantly reduced incomes. Knowing that women are often considerably more in danger of serious violence once they have left abusive partners raises further questions about the double binds inherent in violent intimate relationships.

The title of the book, *Reclaiming Self,* was taken from Jeannette Moldon's description of the process that the group members experience in support groups for abused women. These women recognized that over the years they had accommodated to their partners' wishes, sacrificing their own desires and needs in order to keep safe in the relationship. Learning about the subtle ways that men may intimidate and denigrate women allowed them to re-evaluate what was important to their lives without always sublimating their needs to their partners.

It seems fitting to focus this book on the idea that women can leave abusive relationships, regain their sense of self and begin new lives. Hope is an essential component in the change process. Many women leave abusive partners and establish new violence-free lives.

Other women abused by their partners remain in relationships but struggle every day to maintain a safe place for themselves and their children. Some have not reached a point in their lives when leaving is the preferred alternative; others are all too aware that they would be at serious risk if they attempted to leave. The voices of the women in this book describe not only their trials but also their strengths and successes. We dedicate the book to each of them and to their children.

Chapter Two

How Well do Emergency Shelters Assist Abused Women and their Children?

Leslie M. Tutty and Michael A. Rothery

During the past thirty years, shelters for battered women have become fixtures throughout North America and elsewhere. The first in Canada were Vancouver's Transition House, Ishtar in Langley, B.C., Oasis House (now Calgary Women's Emergency Shelter), Saskatoon's Interval House, and Interval House in Toronto, all of which opened in 1973 (Hebert and Foley, 1997; F. MacLeod, 1989).

Shelters have become a primary resource for protecting assaulted women from violent partners. The latest Transition House Survey (Statistics Canada, 1999/2000) documents that in the year ending March 31, 2000, 96,359 women and dependent children were admitted to 467 shelters (467 of a total of 508 shelters responded to questionnaires). While a minority of these simply needed housing, most (over 80 percent) were leaving abusive homes. Of these, 55 percent were women with dependent children, 73 percent of whom were less than ten years old.

Most Canadian shelters are "first-stage" transition homes, typically offering shelter for an average of three weeks. A smaller number of "second-stage" shelters provide accommodation for six to twelve months, typically to former residents of first-stage shelters for whom a longer-term secure facility is necessary because their abuser remains dangerous to them (Tutty, in press).

In surveys, abused women rate shelters their most effective source of help, more important than traditional service agencies (Bowker and Maurer, 1985; Gordon, 1996). It is clear that the safety and support offered to residents have helped many to leave abusive relationships

(Dziegielewski, Resnick and Krause, 1996; Orava, McLeod and Sharpe, 1996; Tutty, Weaver and Rothery, 1999). Despite this, shelters cannot serve all those who come to their doors, often sending away as many women as they take in or more. In recent statistics from three Alberta shelters for April 1999 through March 2000, a total of 913 women were admitted, but 6668 women were not (Carolyn Goard, personal communication) a ratio of about 1:7. The result for some is homelessness—homeless women are not uncommonly former shelter residents who have failed to find housing (Breton and Bunston, 1992; Charles, 1994).

Not all women leaving abusive relationships require shelter services. The 1999 Statistics Canada national survey found that only 11 percent of women who had experienced spousal violence in the past five years had used a shelter, and the 1993 Violence against Women survey estimated that 13 percent of such women had done so (Rodgers, 1994). In the latter study, most abused women stayed with friends or relatives (77 percent); others moved into a new residence (13 percent) or stayed at a hotel (5 percent). One conclusion to be drawn from such findings is that transition homes are serving those who need them most, providing "options for women who have few options" (Weisz, Taggart, Mockler and Streich, 1994). However, given the above-noted statistics on women who were turned away, it may be that there are simply not enough shelter beds to meet the need.

While shelters are essential, they do not fully meet abused women's needs. Three weeks is a short time for making complicated, fundamentally important decisions. If a woman does decide to leave her partner, she faces myriad other choices about supporting herself and her children and coping with pressure to return to the abusive relationship. When she leaves the shelter she may well be subject to further abuse or threats of abuse, feeling vulnerable and anxious without its protection and support.

Shelter programs have expanded over time. Providing secure accommodation remains their most important purpose, but they also offer counselling, linkages to community agencies, crisis telephone lines, follow-up support for former residents and training for professionals (Davis, Hagen, and Early, 1994; Johnson, Crowley, and Sigler, 1992; Peled and Edleson, 1994). Treatment for children exposed to marital violence is now common, as are prevention programs and even programs to treat abusive partners. Unfortunately, most provincial governments do not fund these additional programs because they are not considered part of core shelter services (Tutty, in press).

In this chapter we review the literature on the efficacy of shelters and present new findings about the experiences of abused women who sought safety in two emergency shelters in urban Alberta centres. This research was designed to improve our understanding of how women decide to seek shelter, their experience living in the transition home, relationships with staff and other residents, and what happens in the four to six months after their shelter stay.

Do Shelters Work?

How effectively do shelters provide assistance to abused women and their children? Several recent Canadian evaluations studied this question. An evaluation of 77 Project Haven shelters (Canada Mortgage and Housing Corporation, 1994), many of which are in rural or First Nations communities, reported that a high proportion of the almost 9,000 residents during a one-year period rated the shelter supports and services as "valuable." Similarly, the 1993 Violence Against Women Survey reported that 81 percent of the women who had used a shelter found it helpful (Rodgers, 1994). Prud'homme (1994) studied 44 Quebec shelters, noting an increased demand for crisis phone line and shelter services, as well as an increase in the number of women and children refused residence because of lack of space.

Several evaluations have also been conducted on second-stage shelters. Russell (1990) reviewed four such Canadian studies, reporting that most residents valued the individual counselling provided to themselves and their children, although, not surprisingly, since needs vary, not all women required the same types or levels of help. The difficulties that women reported in these studies were the unavoidable tensions associated with communal living, including conflicts over children's behaviour and varying child-care practices.

An evaluation of 68 second-stage shelters of the CMHC Canadian Next Step Program (SPR Associates, 1997) concluded that the availability of second-stage housing is a critical factor in the decision not to return to abusive partners. In general, women who had stayed in the second-stage facilities were highly satisfied compared to those who had accessed other assisted housing options. As one would expect, finding affordable accommodation on leaving second-stage facilities was a major concern for the women in the study.

Where Do Women Go After the Shelter?

Several studies have followed women after their shelter stay to identify their needs in facilitating violence-free living. Gondolf and Fisher (1988), Holiman and Schilit, (1991) and the authors of a number of studies on follow-up and advocacy services (Sullivan, 1991; Sullivan and Bybee, 1999; Sullivan and Davidson II, 1991; Sullivan, Tan, Basta, Rumptz and Davidson II, 1992; Sullivan, Campbell, Angelique, Eby and Davidson II, 1994; Tutty, 1993; 1996) all support extending services to abused women beyond their shelter residency.

A significant proportion of women return to their abusive partner after their shelter stay is finished. Cannon and Sparks (1989) reported that in their sample only 50 percent of women who initially declared an intention to leave their partner actually did so. The previously mentioned Canadian survey of 77 Project Haven shelters (Weisz et al., 1994) found that in a large sample of "stays" (9000), 44 percent of the women returned home—27 percent to an unchanged situation and 17 percent to a changed situation (added family counselling or court orders). Women who had been physically abused or threatened were less likely to return to an abusive situation than those who had experienced psychological, emotional or financial abuse.

Why do approximately half of shelter residents return to abusive relationships? One reason is simply that breaking away from an intimate relationship is always complicated and normally requires time; one estimate is that on average four or five attempts to leave precede a permanent split (Giles-Sims, 1983). The observation that leaving is seldom a single decision or event reminds us that returning to an abusive spouse does not represent a failure on the part of the woman or on the part of shelter staff (Okun, 1988).

A lack of resources may force a return to an abusive partner (Dobash et al., 2000; Gondolf and Fisher, 1988; Greaves, Heapy and Wylie, 1988; Prud'homme, 1994; Rothery, Tutty and Weaver, 1999): one quarter of the women in the Project Haven shelter study (Weisz et al., 1994) had difficulty finding affordable and safe housing; women with independent financial resources were less likely to return home after a shelter stay. The lack of safe affordable housing could result in women returning to abusive relationships out of desperation (DeKeseredy and Hinch, 1991).

Furthermore, abuse often continues post-separation, and the hazards associated with leaving are of concern for months (Ellis, 1992), long past the residency allowance in most emergency shelters. Notably, threats against the woman and her children often recur when she leaves the security of the shelter and must re-establish herself in the community where protective resources are not as available (Tutty, 1996). Such threats and the fears they engender may provoke a reunion with an abusive partner (Johnson et al., 1992): without adequate legal protections a woman may conclude that the safest response to escalating risk is to return to a dangerous relationship.

Little is known about what distinguishes women who return home directly from the shelter, those who attempt independent living, and those who successfully manage to live independently. Sometimes, women may simply not see viable options: McDonald et al. (1986) reported that 78 percent of second-stage shelter residents believed that, apart from the transition house, their only choice was to return to the battering relationship. An indication of the extent of their need is the finding that 90 percent of the women in that study had arrived at the second-stage shelter bereft of possessions, clothing or money. After leaving the second-stage shelter, the women were found to have "more internal control and more social independence at six-month follow-up compared to what they experienced when they entered the house" (McDonald, 1989, p.122). In a similar study, Schutte, Bouleige and Malouf (1986) found that women who returned to an abusive relationship were significantly more likely to have low self-esteem and to see themselves as responsible for the violence.

Other researchers have focused on women who return home but must be re-admitted to shelter because their partners became abusive once again. Wilson et al. (1989) found that women who re-entered shelters were more likely to lack income and had more and younger children. Having a supportive network of friends and family, working outside the home and participating in support groups were all factors associated with the cessation of abuse. Each of these factors entails the women being more connected to social supports and less isolated. Interestingly, it was not the amount of earned income that determined a woman's re-admission to a shelter but whether she earned income at all, suggesting that having a job is what matters most. Women who use shelters are often disadvantaged by not being employed (60 percent in Wilson et al., 1989). A successful transition to independent living therefore likely entails job training or upgrading, both of which initially involve spending rather than earning money.

In summary, leaving an abusive spouse requires addressing many issues including housing, employment, child-care, children's emotional reactions to the separation and the myriad pressures of single parenthood. The process of leaving is complex: we are still learning what assists women in making the transition to a violence-free life. Research clearly suggests that shelters are an essential resource—necessary, albeit often not sufficient. However, relatively little research has as yet documented how abused women see these services and in what ways the services do and do not address their needs.

Conversations with Abused Women

The information presented below was gathered in two studies involving two Calgary emergency shelters.[1] Since the studies were conducted with highly similar populations in the same community and since some of the same measures were used in each, it was considered appropriate to combine the information for the purposes of the present analysis.

The aggregate sample comprised a total of 208 women. On admission to the shelter, all completed two standardized self-report scales on the nature and extent of the physical and non-physical abuse from their partners (Hudson, 1992).

A sub-sample of 103 women also completed, on entry to the shelter, the *Impact of Events Scale* (I.E.S.) (Horowitz, Wilner and Alvarez, 1979), a measure developed to assess traumatic responses to a specific event, in this case the incident that led to shelter entry. Trauma reactions are not considered symptoms of psychopathology so much as "normal responses to abnormal occurrences in the lives of these victims" (Gleason, 1993, p. 62). Such reactive symptoms are important because they can interfere in a woman's ability to interact with counsellors and her readiness to make important decisions (Tutty, 1998).

Another sub-group of 102 women was interviewed early in their shelter stay. Of these, 64 were available for follow-up interviews four to six months after leaving the shelter (Tutty, Rothery, Cox and Richardson, 1995; Rothery et al., 1999). The women were first interviewed after they had resided in the shelter for at least a week and a half, so that they had time to get settled and recover somewhat from the initial crisis that led them to seek admission. Each woman was asked to describe her per-ceptions of the shelter staff, facilities and other residents and what was helpful during her stay. At the follow-up interview, each woman was asked to reflect upon her shelter stay and to assess its impact on her current situation. The interviews were transcribed verbatim and analyzed using established qualitative methods (Coleman and Unrau, 1996).

The Women Who Use Emergency Shelters

The 208 women who resided in the shelters were, on average, in their early thirties, ranging in age from sixteen to fifty-nine years. Almost two-thirds had been married or living common-law immediately be-fore shelter entry, with the average length of that relationship being seven years and ranging from one month to thirty years. The partner abuse had occurred for close to the full duration of many of these relationships, an average of six years, ranging from one month to twenty-seven years.

While the majority of the women had sought refuge because of abuse by a male intimate partner, a small number were in residence because of abuse by other family members and incidents with room-mates or neighbours. For example, one woman had been sexually assaulted by a neighbour and no longer felt safe. Other women had been evicted by room-mates (two females, one male); their interview data are included in our analysis but not their scores on the partner abuse scales.

Over half of the 208 women had graduated from high school; one-third of the total had some post-secondary training. Another 81 women

(40 percent) had some high school but had not graduated. Upon entry to the shelter, almost one-quarter of the women reported having no income. The largest proportion (44 percent) had an annual income of less than $10,000 annually. Only 16 women reported an income over $20,000. One-fifth of the residents were employed either full or part time; one-sixth received social assistance and another sixth were homemakers with no personal income. In summary, most were poor, and, if employed, had little income.

Most of the women (87.5 percent) had children; with the average age of the oldest being ten years, ranging from three months to thirty years. A little over half of the women were Caucasian, one-third were Canadian Aboriginal, and a small number were Asian and African-Canadian.

Almost three-quarters of both the women and their partners had been abused as children and/or had been exposed to their parents' marital abuse. Almost three-quarters of the women described their partners as currently abusing substances; a much smaller proportion (14 percent) indicated that they themselves were also doing so. More than one-third of the women were using the shelter for the first time; another third had been residents once before. The remaining third reported a range of from three to twelve previous shelter stays.

The Nature of the Abusive Relationship

In general, the women described abuse that was serious in nature and occurred relatively frequently. Slightly over one-third of the women had required medical attention at some point as a result of being abused. Eighteen women reported having fractured or broken bones, seven reported cuts requiring stitches, six had concussions or head injuries and another six had internal injuries.

Almost three-quarters of the couples had police intervention in the past; more than one-third in the incident that led to their current shelter admission. One-third of the respondents noted that the police had charged their partners. Almost half of the men had a previous criminal record and more than half had been violent towards non-family members. More than a quarter of the women noted that weapons, including guns, knives, axes and wrenches, had been used against them. One woman, who had never actually lived with her partner, described how he told her that he had hidden a gun somewhere in her house. This terrified her, especially since they had young children. Eventually, in two separate incidents, he chased her and the children from the house, brandishing the gun and threatening to kill them, and then himself.

In over half of the families, the women noted that their children had been abused, the majority of the abuse (90 percent) by the current partners. For example, during an argument with his eight-year-old son in the car, one man rolled up the automatic window on the boy's neck. Several of the children had been kidnapped in custody bids, or their fathers had threatened to kidnap them. Predictably, children reacted in troubling ways to such events. Young boys in two families had threatened suicide. One fifteen-year-old adolescent made death threats against his siblings and assaulted his mother.

The average scores on the physical and non-physical abuse scales suggest significant abuse. A sub-set of 57 women self-reported their own abusive behaviours as low in both physical and non-physical abuse, levels that are significantly less than those perpetrated by their partners. These data are solely from the women's perspective, which is not ideal. However, authors such as Szinovacz and Egley (1995) indicate that violence is under-reported by both men and women, but significantly more by men. Thus, utilizing data from the women will be generally more accurate than if we had asked their partners to describe their own abusive behaviours.

On the scale measuring trauma, the women reported reactions that suggest avoidant behaviour (attempting to avoid situations that reminded them of the traumatic event) and trauma in general. These findings are consistent with other research that explored the extent to which abused women experience trauma and that used the same measure (Dutton, 1992; Kemp, Rawlings and Green, 1991).

Although the statistics provide a sense of the serious and traumatic nature of the abuse experienced by the women, comments from the research interviews provide a more vivid understanding of the experiences of living in abusive relationships.[2] In truth, many of the assaults were brutal. Women received death threats against themselves and their children, especially if they were considering leaving the relationship. A number were beaten while pregnant. Others described having had "lots of broken bones," being "flipped over, smacked on the head and punched in the crotch," being thrown out of a car travelling at highway speed. One partner deliberately broke his partner's arm; another, after surgery, deliberately kicked his wife in the site of her incision. Another man forced his partner to strip off her clothes and walk barefoot on a floor strewn with broken glass.

Women were raped by their partners, with almost half reporting sexual abuse in their relationship—for a small number it was a weekly or daily occurrence. On returning home, one man would inspect his partner's sexual parts because of extreme jealousy. We should note that we did not explicitly ask the women about sexual assaults and, in other research, it has been found that women tend not to disclose this easily. Thus the women likely under-reported in this research.

Partners were stalking 17 women. Each of these had been separated for two years or more. These relationships had all involved serious physical abuse, many with marital rape and threats of murder. One woman was kidnapped and taken to the U.S. by her partner. Another partner forced his common-law wife to tattoo a distinctive mark on her face so that he could locate her if she left him. Yet another woman was kidnapped with her young child and held captive in a basement for a month, fed only sporadically.

Several of the women had to relocate in an effort to escape such abusive partners:

> My ex-boyfriend was abusive. We were living in [another province]; we had been together almost seven years. He got a five-year prison sentence [for abusing her] and he only did five months. I left and went to a shelter in Ontario where I stayed for six weeks; then I went to second stage housing for almost seven months. In the meantime he was threatening my little brother that he'd kill him if he didn't let him know where I was. So my little brother told him. My brother let me know I was in danger. I left and came to Calgary.

> It was the fear of being killed or having my kids hurt that made me leave my house finally. I went to a shelter in Quebec at first. We looked at my options, restraining orders and stuff like that. We thought that would not be a good enough deterrent for him. It would be more of a challenge—something that would make him worse.

The serious, degrading and intentional nature of the abuse exemplifies "patriarchal terrorism" as described by Johnson (1995) in Chapter One. The need for refuge when the potential for such treatment is present is indisputable.

The Shelter Experience

Do emergency shelters meet the needs of abused women? One goal of the current research was to discover the extent to which the residents felt that the shelter provided the help they needed. Our respondents identified the major benefits as emotional support from shelter staff, safety, support from other residents, child support programs, information and connections to community resources. On the negative side, some women raised concerns about the available counselling and aspects of living communally with a large number of other women and children. Each of these concerns is elaborated in the following sections using the resident's words.

Emotional Support from Shelter Staff

Asked about what was most helpful in the shelter, virtually all of the respondents mentioned counselling and described the shelter workers as caring and supportive. Shelter staff seemed busy, but they typically found time to talk to residents, often taking the initiative to do so. The women described them as skilled and respectful listeners:

> I feel comfortable with them. They empathize with you, not sympathize. They're understanding. They've given me reassurance that I am a good mom. I have done the right thing. They keep giving me credit for what I have done, even if it's just one small thing.

> The counsellors have been very supportive of my decisions, very supportive of me and have guided me when I started to get a little panicky. Somebody would say "okay, this is what will happen, you don't have to worry about that today, and in three days then we'll do this." I got a lot of affirmation through the decisions that I have made, so it was "yes, I have done the right thing." That was really very helpful. I needed to hear that I was doing really well.

A number of residents mentioned how important it was to have staff available twenty-four hours a day. Others spoke of the value of being in a setting where they felt comfortable enough to relax and had time to think about the decisions they had to make. One woman said, for example, "I came here depressed, upset, mixed up, confused, and just being here I was able to relax and able to process my own thoughts. And the shelter staff are able to sit down and talk through thoughts."

The women felt comfortable expressing their feelings to the workers, and a number mentioned that the staff were non-judgemental. This objectivity was seen as crucial, enabling women to talk openly about their continuing love for their partners or their conflicting feelings about returning to him. As one resident commented, "They don't judge you. If you get talked into going back into the relationship, they're still here for you."

Safety

A critical aspect of the shelter mentioned by almost half of the women was its safety, something many had rarely experienced before. Several commented that they were able to sleep well for the first time in years.

> When I first came it was kind of scary. The kids were confused, didn't know what was going on. But as time went by, I felt

safer. I mean, I've gone out maybe three times since. I just feel safe in here. If I don't have to go out, I won't.

I feel safer. It's a violence-free place and there's no verbal abuse.

Connecting with Other Shelter Residents

Thirty-four women commented on the benefits of living with other abused women. Some found that they could confide in other residents more than they could with friends, family members and shelter staff. They believed that other abused women could understand their feelings and their problems better than those who have never been in abusive situations.

Further benefits with respect to other residents included exchanging information, advice and practical support. One respondent commented, "The residents that live here also—they back each other up on a lot of things. If someone's depressed or busy with another kid, or whatever—they all help each other out. It's good that way." Another woman noted that, "The other residents will let you in on stuff, there's a lot of organizations for single moms, stuff like that." Others elaborated on this theme:

> I relate to the women really well. We're all going through the same thing. There are some women that are really strong, I was talking to one this morning. She's left her situation, she says "I don't need an intake worker, I just need some money to get going on my feet, I'm not going back there." I'm glad she's my roommate because she gives strength.

> Being in here has been very positive for me, not because of the safety factor, not only because there's a counsellor, but because I've had the ability for the first time in my life to sit down with a bunch of other women, which I've never done before, and tell them all about me.

Information and Connections to Community Resources

A number of women described the value of the information and referrals they received at the shelter. This included information about their legal rights, resources in the community and various aspects of abuse, as well as concrete needs. As one resident commented, "I didn't know about going for a restraining order, calling for the police, what number is legal aid, legal guidance, and so how could I know if I wasn't here?" Another woman appreciated the staff's patience in going over large amounts of information with her. She said, "You're very emotional when you come in; you're not very clear, so the information is very helpful."

A number of the women expressed gratitude for the shelter's connection with a local subsidized housing agency that gives priority to shelter residents. Such access to housing made it much easier for them to leave the shelter to live independently. Several interviewees suggested that information could be made more accessible. One woman commented that it would be useful to have all the resources listed in a binder for women in the shelter.

Child Support Program

Women with children were generally pleased with the shelter child support program. Their children enjoyed the activities in the shelter, felt safe and liked the child support counsellors. The women also commented on the importance of having someone care for their children at some point during the day so that they could have time to relax and reflect. Several mothers would have liked more child-care, and one mentioned that she would have liked more activities for older children, especially teenagers. Several mothers were appreciative of the help they received in parenting their children.

Concerns Regarding the Shelter

Despite the overall positive nature of the comments, residents expressed concerns about several aspects of the shelter. The availability of shelter staff, while viewed positively by the majority, was the most commonly expressed concern raised by others. Residents mentioned that the counsellors were too busy and that, although these staff were supportive, it was difficult to talk to them in the office, with so many distractions, particularly the crisis telephone line. As one woman explained, "It's frustrating at times because I always feel like I'm interrupting. It's busy, and when I'm there talking the phone's ringing, the door's buzzing, and it's maddening because you don't really have their undivided attention." Others had a similar perception that resulted in their not seeking assistance because of being afraid of interrupting. A number wished that the staff would approach the residents to inquire about how they are doing:

> They [shelter staff] need somebody that is on top of things all the time. If they see somebody's a bit emotional, they take them aside right then and there and deal with it. Not wait for the women to come to them. They have to go to the women, and not a clinical approach, not this psychologist kind-of ... but a more humane approach. Like use terms that a lot of these women can understand, maybe talk a little slang, and throw in

a couple of cuss words. You have to know how to approach these people for them to build up trust with the workers and really open up to them.

They don't come out to see if you want to talk. They expect you to go to them. They just don't seem interested in our problems and if we have a problem, we won't actually go and attempt to talk. Something else will come up. Somebody else will come in and interrupt. They just let them sit there, instead of saying, "Well, you can come back in twenty minutes," or whatever.

Several mentioned that it was confusing to have different workers and tiring to have to repeatedly tell their stories. A few also received conflicting advice. One woman commented, "I get confused because one person says this and another is saying this, and another is nice and trying to explain." A different resident found it difficult to have to tell her story "from scratch" over and over because the staff rotates through shift changes. She similarly noted that different counsellors sometimes gave her contradictory advice.

One woman strongly expressed her desire for crisis counselling on shelter entry:

I think there's a real weak point in shelters that needs to be addressed. When you walk into a shelter, you've been completely traumatized. You walk in there, they tell you to have a good night's sleep. Within the next couple of days they'll have a counsellor to talk to you.... I truly believe the minute you walk in there you should be debriefed and counselled immediately. Just given a chance to pour your heart out. You don't need a bed to go to sleep in; you need somebody to talk to because you have finally made the decision to walk out. That critical crisis counselling is not in place and I feel a lot of the reason a lot of women go back is because of that.

A small number of negative comments were about specific shelter staff. One resident noted, "There's a few of the night staff that I don't care for. They're just not easy to talk to." One found some workers judgmental towards her partner, another that a particular staff crisis counsellor seemed to "look down" on her.

A number of the concerns were expressed with respect to difficulties in communal living. A common issue in many shelters is the chore system. Since shelters receive limited funding, most require the residents to help with cleaning, and sometimes cooking. The residents complained that some women do not do their fair share of the work:

Some of the people don't do what they're supposed to. There was one day that I missed [chores], and then I did two the next day, but it seems that some of the girls don't do that and get out of it. It's hard to control everyone. You don't want to be a cop, but if there was a way to make sure that everyone does her chores.

I found some of the rules a little frustrating. I understand, but they're frustrating.

Several women were concerned about the behaviour of a small number of residents. It appeared that the needs of these women were too great for the staff to meet, leaving others feeling unsafe and worried about their children. The behaviours of concern included alcohol and drug abuse, poor personal hygiene, and erratic, angry and sometimes volatile behaviour:

I realize they [shelter staff] have to make judgment calls at times. The state the women were in that night I would have let them stay the night, but the next day when they were in the same space, I would have referred them to detox or a substance abuse agency. I didn't want my boys seeing them in that state, because we're supposed to be here feeling at home and at ease, but then you were walking around the hallways seeing them and I just didn't like it."

There seemed to be a high level of anger that was really easily provoked. Some people were very dramatic; like they lived on drama. [There was a lot of conflict?] Yeah. One woman went screaming down the hall swearing her head off, and I mean I was scared.

A number perceived conflict between some residents as problematic:

Sometimes it gets frustrating because not everyone gets along and it's not really the shelter's fault.

I really don't like being here. I don't like sharing a room with three other women. I feel a lot more comfortable with the staff (half laugh) than I do with the rest of the group. I'll be happy to go, let's put it that way.

Others were concerned that some mothers were not managing their children's behaviour or were neglecting them.

They should give a crash course to the young mothers. Even though they're from abusive situations they should spend more time with their children.

The moms don't look after their own kids. In there, they more or less let the kids run wild. The kids would dump a glass of apple juice on the floor, and the mom would just walk away. Let whoever's on late night clean it up.

There are some children that have been neglected, and I don't think that situation is really handled. I don't know what role the shelter is supposed to play but there have been some moms that I'm sure shouldn't have their children.

Post-Shelter Relationship with Partner

Almost two-thirds of the women (64 or 61 percent) were available for a follow-up interview between four to six months after they had lived in the shelter. Although whether or not they returned to their abusive partner is only one indication of the impact of the shelter, it does provide important information about their safety. Also, the question of whether women return to ex-partners is continually raised, so this aspect of how the women were doing seemed a worthwhile focus.

At the second interviews, the majority (90 percent) were living independently of their abusive partners. Of these, about one-third had some contact, mostly because of child visitation. Twenty-four women (38 percent) had no contact with their previous partners: over half of these women lived virtually in hiding, fearing that their partners would learn of their whereabouts. Three women had received threatening phone calls, two from men in jail, one of whom was on trial for murder. One woman who had not had contact met her assaultive partner at the funeral of her brother, a suspected murder victim. He badly beat her and she sought refuge once again in the shelter. Three women were living independently but were considering reuniting. In each of these cases, the partner had received professional treatment (two for substance abuse, one for counselling).

Six women of the total of 64 (9 percent) had returned and currently lived with their assaultive partner, and, although no one mentioned the abuse recurring, two were ambivalent about remaining in the relationship. Ten additional women (16 percent) had reconciled, but then left the relationship. In all but one of these cases, the abuse had re-occurred. One woman's partner had again threatened her life with a firearm and was arrested. One woman had a serious fight with her partner and, in her attempt to flee, accidentally ran over him with her car. He has since threatened her about her testimony with respect to that incident. One woman became involved in a new relationship that became abusive; four women are in new relationships that have not become violent, although one woman was still being pressured to return to her previously abusive partner.

The Context of Shelters for Abused Women

The current study was proposed as a much-needed evaluation of emergency shelters from the viewpoint of residents, both during their residency and four to six months later. The responses to the standardized measures offered startling details about the severity of the abuse. The interviews provided the opportunity to identify the most salient issues faced by abused women and the extent to which the services addressed these new or ongoing problems.

Overall, the women agreed that the shelter addressed many of their needs and that the experience was often life-altering. Their concerns about the shelter were relatively few in number. Nonetheless, the residents raised important questions about how shelter staff respond to the seemingly never-ending stream of women who rotate through their facility. Shelters are no longer the grass-roots refuges of the early 1970s, but have become professionalized and bureaucratized. According to the respondents, most shelter counsellors respond respectfully and helpfully. However, the residents' views that the staff were often coping with competing demands such as dealing with crisis calls and in-house incidents and enforcing the chore schedule is consistent with other research about burnout and vicarious trauma in shelter personnel (Tutty and Rothery, 1997). This is not meant to excuse insensitive counselling but to acknowledge that the staff is institutionalized in the same way as residents and all react to the closed-in shelter environment. For example, with the need for shelter security systems, both the staff and residents are locked in. If the shelter is threatened, all experience the same fear. Such complex organizations require careful attention to the needs of all.

The follow-up interviews with previous shelter residents provide an important perspective that is seldom offered. However, consistent with the literature, these narratives remind us that abuse often does not end after a woman leaves a relationship. Women with children often have no choice but to have at least limited contact with their former partners. Those who desire no contact may have their privacy repeatedly invaded if their ex-partner is determined to find them. Women who have been stalked by partners have few alternatives, one being to flee from province to province utilizing shelter services as they go, in the hope that they can find a place to live independently where they will be safe from harassment.

The belief that most women return to abusive partnerships is contradicted by the previous shelter residents who were available for a follow-up interview. Only one-quarter of the women had returned to their previous partners, and most of these left when another abusive incident occurred. A minority had entered new relationships, most of which were not abusive.

We can only guess at the reasons why the proportion of women living independently at follow-up was so much higher than in previous studies, most of which were conducted in the 1980s. It may be that only women living away from partners were willing to participate in the second interviews. Alternatively, perhaps shelter staff now better assist women to make and maintain a decision to leave. Nonetheless, the expectation that abused women necessarily either return to abusive partners or develop new relationships with abusive men is not consistent with the experiences of this, albeit small, group of previous shelter residents.

It seems fitting to end this chapter with the voices of the shelter residents describing their thoughts about the shelter in general. In the interviews, the majority of women commented that the shelter was essential. A number noted that without their shelter stay, they would not have left abusive partners:

> If it weren't for a shelter, I don't know where I'd be ... probably on the roadside.

> If it hadn't been for the shelter, I would still be there. That was the start of realizing that I am not his punching bag. I am not his property. He doesn't own me, and he doesn't have the right to treat me as a prisoner.

> The kids love it, the kids literally love it. The shelter has made a really big difference to me. They have given me a lot a lot of strength and support.

> I had expected that the shelter was just a place to stay. I have been surprised at all of the help I have received.

> Everybody here cares. You're allowed to hurt, to feel. You're allowed to say what you feel [crying]. That's important. It makes me feel stronger.

> If it wasn't for the shelter, where would I be? I'd probably be dead.

Overwhelmingly, these comments reflect the importance of the shelter experience to its residents.

Notes

1. The Family Violence Prevention Division of Health Canada and the Social Sciences and Humanities Research Council of Canada funded the research projects. Thanks to Gillian Cox/Weaver and Cindy Ogden who conducted the interviews.
2. Identifying features have been disguised to protect confidentiality.

Chapter Three

"His Sentence is My Freedom"

Processing Domestic Violence Cases in the Winnipeg Family Violence Court

Jane Ursel

> "Domestic Terrorist Hit With 25 Year Sentence"
> The previous day Madame Justice Keyser made legal history in sentencing a Winnipeg man to 25 years imprisonment for the sustained and brutal abuse of his wife and children over a period of 11 years. The crown prosecutor, Mr. Ken Champange was quoted as saying that he ... "could find only one other non-murder case in Canadian history involving a 25-year sentence. It was given to a B.C. sex abuser." (*Winnipeg Free Press*, May 31, 2001, p.1)

This case made headlines because of the severity of the abuse and the unusual sentence. Rarely are wife abuse offenders sentenced to more than several months of incarceration. While the sentence and the severity of the abuse may make the case remarkable, there are many aspects of Mr. and Mrs. Ash's[1] life together and their involvement in the criminal justice system that are typical of wife abuse cases.

I begin this chapter by considering what is typical about the Ash case rather than what is unique, because this illustrates in a very dramatic manner the complexities of wife abuse cases and the challenges that they pose to the criminal justice system (CJS). I will argue that the traditional paradigm of justice is not adequate to the challenge of such cases. I then describe a specialized response within the justice system, the Winnipeg Family Violence Court, and assess its ability to respond more effectively.

What are the characteristics of the Ash case that are typical of domestic assaults that come to the attention of the police and the courts in Winnipeg?

- Throughout the eleven years of marriage the abuse was recurrent and escalating.
- The Ash's had three children and a fourth child by a prior relationship.
- The children were direct victims of abuse as well as witnesses to their mother's abuse.
- Mrs. Ash was systematically isolated from her family and friends.
- Mrs. Ash had a low income and few resources to call on other than the police.
- Between 1987 and 1998, Mrs. Ash called for police help five times.
- Mr. Ash was arrested on serious assault charges each time, specifically April 1988, June 1991, November 1991, August 1993 and, finally, in June of 1998.
- All arrests prior to 1998 ended in "stays of proceedings"[2] because Mrs. Ash did not testify.
- Mr. Ash had a prior record for acts of violence before his marriage.
- Mrs. Ash and her children had used shelter services as part of her escape plan.

This familiar litany of characteristics reminds us that women and children caught in a violent family often have great difficulty breaking free. Isolation from support is a common tactic of abusive partners, leaving the wife dependent and unable to leave. While the presence of children is often a powerful motivator for women to leave, they are also powerful tools of manipulation for the abuser: "If you call the police the children will pay ... if you testify in court you will never see the kids again." Mrs. Ash had attempted to flee the relationship five times before being successful. Escaping a violent relationship is typically a slow and painful process. It is this characteristic of repeated unsuccessful attempts to leave that challenges the justice system and points to the need for a new approach.

The traditional paradigm of criminal justice is ill-equipped to respond to domestic violence cases for a number of reasons. First, the CJS "is organized around discrete incidents and official investment in incidents is shaped by their legal seriousness and probabilities of conviction ... but domestic violence typically involves multiple incidents, sometimes of escalating seriousness, with little physical evidence and few witnesses" (Worden, 2000, p. 233). Second, because of the adversarial nature of the criminal justice process it is assumed that "both sides" are committed to winning "their case," i.e., that the victim has the same interest as the crown attorney—public conviction and punishment. However, victims of domestic violence have diverse motivations for seeking CJS intervention (Ford, 1991; Ford and Regoli, 1993; Ursel, 1998). As well, many victims face collateral legal issues such as divorce, custody and child support proceedings. In short, domestic violence cases typically involve a process rather than a discrete incident. They are complex and messy rather than being straightforward evidentiary matters.

It is this "disconnect" between the characteristics of a traditional justice approach and the realities of domestic violence that has led to questions about the CJS as an appropriate intervention in domestic violence matters. The measures of success for the traditional paradigm do not "fit" domestic violence cases. If arrests don't deter future violence, should we arrest? Mr. Ash was arrested four times and each time, after release, continued his pattern of violence. If prosecution does not result in conviction, should we prosecute? Winnipeg crown attorneys attempted to prosecute Mr. Ash four times unsuccessfully. It was twelve years after his first arrest that they finally succeeded. I will argue that, rather than discarding the CJS as an intervention, we should develop a new approach that better fits the complex nature of domestic violence cases. To inform this discussion, I combine debates within the literature on criminal justice interventions in domestic violence with data from the Winnipeg Family Violence Court (FVC).[3]

Toward a New Approach to Justice

Over the last eighteen years, a series of policy changes have been introduced in the criminal justice system in Winnipeg.[4] These changes were designed to make the system more responsive to the special challenges posed by domestic violence cases.

- 1983: The Attorney General of Manitoba issued a directive to the police forces in Manitoba to charge, stating that when there are reasonable and probable grounds to indicate that a crime has occurred the police must charge regardless of the relationship between the victim and the accused;
- 1986: The creation of the Women's Advocacy Program to assist women whose partners have been charged, to assess the victim's risk, to develop safety plans and to prepare the women for court when necessary;
- 1990: The development of the specialized criminal court for family violence cases, the Family Violence Court (FVC), which provides specialized prosecutors and designated courts for intake, screening, preliminary hearings and trials;
- 1992: The creation of a Specialized Correctional program within Community Probations which provided specialized counsellors to run batterers treatment groups for court mandated offenders;
- 1993: Winnipeg Police Service introduce their domestic violence policy referred to by the press as "Zero Tolerance";

- 1997: Expansion of the specialized prosecutors' Family Violence Unit so that crown attorneys can follow cases from bail hearings to Provincial Court to Court of Queens Bench and Court of Appeal;
- 2000: Winnipeg Police Service create the position of Domestic Violence Coordinator;
- 2000: Manitoba Corrections introduced a special unit for domestic violence offenders at Headingley prison; and
- 2001: Winnipeg Police Service introduces a new pilot project focused on early intervention in domestic violence cases.

There is some indication that each of the above reforms has made the CJS more accessible to women and children at risk. Evidence from a national transition home survey indicates that Manitoba women were more likely than women in other provinces to call the police during a violent assault upon them (see Figure 3-1). Furthermore, Manitoba police were much more likely to arrest the accused when called to the scene of a domestic violence incidence (see Figure 3-2).[5]

Despite evidence that more women at risk are accessing services within the criminal justice system, there are still barriers. Historically, measures of success within the CJS have been one-dimensional, focusing on "outcome" rather than "process," and mired in the "single-incident" framework. This framework encourages police officers, crown

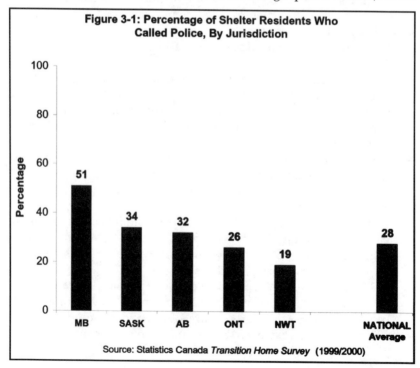

Figure 3-1: Percentage of Shelter Residents Who Called Police, By Jurisdiction

Source: Statistics Canada *Transition Home Survey* (1999/2000)

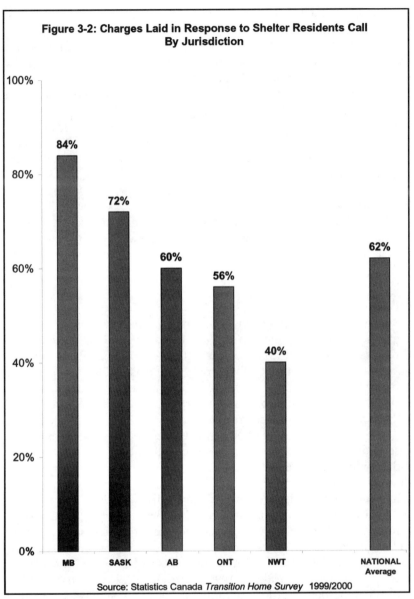

Figure 3-2: Charges Laid in Response to Shelter Residents Call By Jurisdiction

Source: Statistics Canada *Transition Home Survey* 1999/2000

attorneys and judges to view their role as a single, preferably decisive intervention. However, survival and recovery are seldom single-event propositions. A single police response, court appearance or stay in a women's shelter does not miraculously change the complex web of love, fear, dependency and intimidation woven into the fabric of an abused woman's life. While policy reforms are necessary, they are not sufficient—equally important are the definitions of success and the culture of work within the CJS. These must change in order to do justice for these families.

The most important change would be for CJS staff to understand the paradox of dealing with family violence. Circumstances often make CJS intervention a matter of life or death, yet this intervention is profoundly limited. A quick police response, a denied bail request or a jail sentence may be critical in preventing a domestic homicide; however, such outcomes cannot, in and of themselves, prevent the cycle of abuse. This suggests that the CJS must redefine success. If we change the goals of intervention from conviction (a one-dimensional outcome) to redressing dangerous power imbalances (a complex process of empowerment), then possibly the CJS could offer women at risk meaningful interventions.

To explore the challenge domestic violence cases present to the CJS, the next sections examine the different components of the justice system in the sequence in which people most frequently encounter them: police, prosecutors and courts.

Policing

In Winnipeg, the policy changes for police were initiated by the charging directive in 1983 and the zero tolerance policy in 1993. In each case, the message was that domestic assaults are serious criminal matters, and police should arrest when there are reasonable and probable grounds rather than considering the violence as a private matter because it was between two intimate partners. The impact of these new policies was dramatic (see Figure 3-3).

Pro-arrest policies are often controversial because they limit police discretion. Critics of these policies argue that police should be provided with greater discretion than zero tolerance or pro-arrest policies permit. Buel (1988) and Stark (1993) have noted that we must consider why pro-arrest policies were introduced in the first place and whether the conditions, to date, suggest that they are no longer necessary. A number of researchers have documented the often diverse attitudes of police officers about domestic violence (e.g., Homant and Kennedy, 1985; Dolon, Hendricks and Meagher, 1986; Breci and Simons, 1987; Friday, Metzgar and Walters, 1991). Further, these and other studies indicate that police attitudes influence police response and action (Rigakos and Bonneycastle, 1998; Dobash and Dobash, 1979; Ericson and Baranek, 1982). McGillivray and Comaskey (1996) documented the particular concerns of Aboriginal women about police attitudes. Women reported experiences in which police did not believe them, judged them and blamed them for their own victimization: "I've always called the police. As a matter of fact, one time when I called the police, the staff sergeant was upset with me. He says, 'I'm getting pretty upset

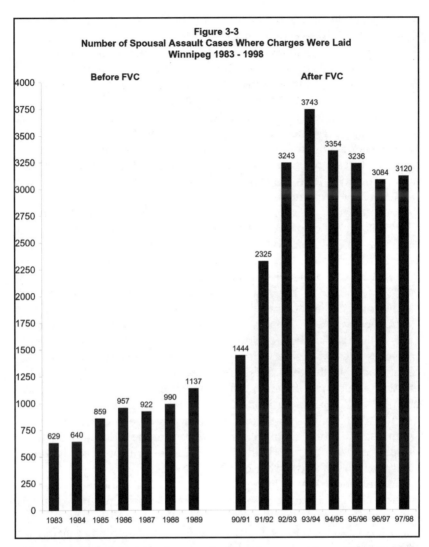

Figure 3-3
Number of Spousal Assault Cases Where Charges Were Laid
Winnipeg 1983 - 1998

with you, you're always phoning, calling here, you're getting to be a bloody nuisance.… I should charge you for harassing, phoning here all the time'" (McGillvrary and Comaskey, 1986, p. 96).

"Low discretion" or "no discretion" policies are supposed to take the "attitude" out of action. Let's return to the Ash case. The police responded and arrested Mr. Ash repeatedly over an eleven-year period, only to see the court cases fall apart because Mrs. Ash did not testify. Such patterns are discouraging for police officers. What might have happened if they had become cynical and concluded that there was no point in arresting in the final instance because the case would be unsuccessful, just as it had been the four previous times? Such an attitude, while understandable, could have been lethal. Thus, until there is a full appreciation of the repetitive and escalating nature of family violence, sufficient to outweigh the fatigue and cynicism of officers repeatedly called to the same household, it is necessary to have policies that separate attitude from action. No one could have predicted that the arrest of Mr. Ash in 1998 would be the decisive event that would lead to a new life for Mrs. Ash and her children. Thus, each arrest must carry the same message to the victim and the offender regardless of outcome in the courts. The victim must know that the police will respond, will conduct a serious investigation and will take action; the offender must know that abuse is a crime and that there will be serious consequences.

Another debate about police intervention is also about outcome. The rise and fall of pro-arrest arguments in North America have been tied to a single measure of success, congruent with the traditional paradigm of justice: Did the arrest prevent future violence (Worden, 2000)? This one-dimensional measure of success is inadequate to the complex nature of the crime of family violence and the diverse motivations of the victim who calls the police (Ursel, 1998; Sullivan, Basta, Tan, and Davidson II, 1992). Some researchers and most advocates maintain that the most important reason for police response and a pro-arrest policy is safety (Jaffe, Reitzel, Hastings and Austin, 1991; Harrell and Smith, 1998). Safety as a measure of success is both congruent with the police officers' professional mandate "to keep the peace" and the victim's motivations at the time of the actual or anticipated assault: to prevent the particular attack or to prevent its escalation. The Winnipeg data indicate that over 80 percent of the domestic calls to the police are made by the victim herself, and her primary motivation is safety for herself and/or her children (Ursel, 2001).

Women typically call the police either during an ongoing or anticipated assault. The current zero tolerance policy requires that the police arrest and remove the alleged offender, thus providing an effective short-term deterrent to escalating violence. Understanding that domestic violence is, by its nature, a recurring crime with a marked tendency to escalation, the issue of safety should be paramount. Vulnerable family members use rapid police response to correct a power imbalance between themselves and their assaultive partner. The person who calls the police for protection may choose not to "use" the rest of the criminal justice system, declining to testify as a witness in court, for example. Yet, some researchers (Schmidt and Steury, 1989) cite a failure to convict as indicative of the failure of police policy. However, we need to ask why police intervention should be considered "unsuccessful" and "inappropriate" if it successfully prevents an escalation of violence.

Applying the same measure of success to our shelters and crisis services would mean that these interventions should also deter future violence. We would have to conclude that shelters have failed since studies have documented that over 60 percent of the shelter residents return to their abusive partner and sustain subsequent abuse (MacLeod, 1987). We do not use "deterrence" as a measure of success to evaluate our social services because we understand the cyclic and recurring nature of family violence. We know that women's struggles to deal with abusive partners are seldom resolved by a single stay in a shelter or a single call to the police; however, some researchers such as Schmidt and Sherman (1993) still use this one-dimensional measure to evaluate police interventions. While service providers recognize it as unreasonable to expect a single intervention, in a single case, at a single point in time to "solve" such complex problems, there is an underlying assumption that greater accessibility to support/intervention programs will, over time, reduce victims' vulnerability. It took five arrests before Mrs. Ash was able to escape her domestic nightmare.

A final criticism of police intervention in domestic violence cases is the issue of class bias. The Winnipeg data indicates that more people with low income are arrested and prosecuted for domestic violence offences than people in other income categories. Canadian sociologist Laureen Snider is concerned about the over-criminalization of people with low incomes and visible minorities. "Lower income, visible minority and Aboriginal women have paid a heavy price for mandatory criminalization. It is primarily their communities ... that are targeted for enhanced surveillance" (Snider, 1998, p.146).

The concern about class bias and excessive surveillance is fuelled by researchers' and service providers' observations that police intervention is seldom anyone's first choice. Canadian historian Carol Strange (1995, p. 301) noted that "historical evidence of battered wives' strategies confirms that women avoid the criminal courts whenever alternatives are available." In most cases, this is simple to understand. If we were being abused and had some way of both stopping that abuse and preventing its recurrence without calling the police, that would probably be our first choice. This would especially be so if we could keep the matter from public, and often unsympathetic, scrutiny.

Yet every year in Winnipeg, a city of 670,000 people, thousands of women call the police requesting protection from abusive partners. As mentioned previously, the victim makes the majority (82 percent) of these calls herself. In addition, over 1,500 women applied for a protection order in the first year that the new *Domestic Violence and Stalking Protection, Prevention and Compensation Act* was enforced. Even with the recent option of a specific civil remedy, the calls to the Winnipeg police have increased in the past year. The Winnipeg police recorded over

14,000 calls of a domestic nature in 2000.[6] Almost two-thirds of the police calls (60 percent) come from two districts that have a high ratio of individuals with low incomes and Aboriginal households.

Given that, in most cases, the police are not the preferred source of help, why do so many women contact the police? Two factors may explain this. First, thousands of women at risk have no access to alternatives; they cannot afford lawyers or personal bodyguards. Nor do they have wealthy relatives who can finance "a great escape." Most women who use police services to stop violence are women with little or no income, although not only poor women call the police. The second factor explaining calls to the police is imminent danger. The Canadian Violence Against Women survey found that a "battered woman's decision to involve police is related to the severity of the violence and whether children were involved.... A woman is three times as likely to call the police if she had children who witnessed the violence, four times as likely if she was injured, and five times as likely if she fears her life is in danger" (Johnson, 1995, pp. 142, 144). McGillivray and Comaskey report similar findings in their interviews with Aboriginal women in Winnipeg: "The most frequent reason for calling police was fear for her safety and that of her children" (1996, p. 95).

The controversy over appropriate police intervention in low-income communities is long-standing. Low-income and/or Aboriginal accused have expressed concern that they are more likely to "suffer" police intervention for behaviour that would not result in police intervention in a middle-class community (Snider, 1998; Goldstein, 1977). This is supported by data from the criminal courts, including the Winnipeg FVC, which consistently show that low-income and Aboriginal people are over-represented in the criminal justice system. Notably though, low-income and/or Aboriginal victims typically utilize the police as their major source of help (McGillivray and Comaskey, 1998; LaRocque, 1993; McEvoy and Daniluk, 1995). Thus, the over-representation of low-income and/or Aboriginal people in the FVC is likely a reflection of the limited resources available to actual or potential victims. Limiting or removing that support would result in many more women's lives being at risk, particularly women of low income or Aboriginal background.

In assessing how great that risk would be, information on the nature of the crime and the prior record rate of the accused is helpful in gauging how potentially dangerous an accused could be. Two important risk indicators are whether the accused used or threatened use of a weapon and whether he had a prior record of violence. Using these criteria, the Winnipeg FVC data suggest that there is a high degree of risk when police are called. Nineteen percent of the accused had used or threatened use of a weapon, and 76 percent of the individuals arrested had a prior record. Furthermore, the majority of the prior records were for crimes of violence: 73 percent for crimes against persons, of which 46 percent were for prior domestic assaults. These findings suggest that Winnipeg women had substantial reason to fear for their safety and that their calls to the police were calls for protection.

In conclusion, the case in favour of zero tolerance or pro-arrest policies is primarily the case for protection. Debates about whether or not arrests deter future violence do not speak to the most pressing problem of deterring the escalation of ongoing or imminent violence, the outcome measure most appropriate to assessing police intervention. No service other than the police has all of the essential components for providing protection in high-risk situations. It provides twenty-four-hour, seven-days-a-week service; a rapid response system; response units trained in high-risk interventions; a response that ensures separation of victim and accused, with restraining orders if the accused is released; and a response without prejudice (no discretion). The zero tolerance policy is the Winnipeg Police Service's attempt to ensure that all five components are operating when a person at risk calls the police.

Prosecution

Along with the expansion of police pro-arrest policies throughout North America has come a complementary move to encourage more rigorous prosecution of domestic violence offenders. As a result, many jurisdictions have developed pro-prosecution and/or no-drop policies. Despite these policies, even recent studies report rates of case attrition through stays of proceedings of almost 50 percent (Davis, Smith and Nickles, 1998; Ursel, 2001).

Prosecutors consistently explain the high rate of stays of proceedings in terms of victim ambivalence. They consider themselves very dependent on the victim's testimony because domestic assaults seldom involve witnesses and do not necessarily provide a rich source of material evidence. The concept of the "uncooperative witness" is derived from the assumption that the victims ought to share the prosecutor's objective of conviction. An implied corollary is that victims who fail to cooperate forfeit their entitlement to the benefits of the legal system (Stanko, 1981–82). As Worden wrote:

> Researchers and victim advocates have questioned both assumptions. First, some argue that prosecution could, and ought to, encompass a wider array of objectives, including victim safety (which might be promoted by the offenders legal entanglement, independent of the ultimate outcome), communicating to offenders the unacceptability of the violent act, and investing victims with greater power and agency in dealing

with violent partners (Fields, 1978; Lerman, 1981; Mickish and
Schoen, 1988). (Worden, 2000, p. 238)

Throughout North America, two strategies have been introduced
to bridge the gap between prosecutors' roles and expectations and
victims' needs and interests. The first approach, frequently referred to
as the "no-drop" policy, attempts to bridge the gap in the favour of
traditional prosecutorial goals. This model works within the traditional justice paradigm in which success is measured by conviction: it
directs prosecutors to proceed with the prosecution regardless of the
victim's needs or wishes. The emphasis is upon more thorough investigation and greater reliance on expert witnesses and material evidence
rather than victim/witness evidence. This option has been adopted
more frequently in the United States than in Canada (Worden, 2000).

The second strategy, practised within the Winnipeg FVC, attempts
to bridge the gap between prosecutors and victims through the pursuit
of a new approach to justice intervention. This approach takes as its
starting point that victim's needs and concerns should guide the course
of justice intervention. This orientation encourages prosecutors and
other personnel in the justice system to define "success" in terms of
meeting the complex needs of the victim and her family rather than
seeking conviction as the most desired outcome. It marks a radical
departure from the traditional justice paradigm, providing more degrees of freedom to the prosecutor and more flexibility in court personnel's ability to respond to the stated needs of the victim and her family.

The critical first step in changing the justice response in Winnipeg
was acknowledging that the existing system wasn't working. In search
of a more responsive system, specialization was introduced. The "short-
hand" for this expanding process of specialization is the Family Violence Court, which began operating in September 1990. The first major
component is a specialized unit in the prosecutor's office with designated crown attorneys who exclusively prosecute family violence matters from initial bail hearings to trial.

Second, a Women's Advocacy program, composed of counsellors,
works with women whose partners have been charged to develop
safety plans and provides information on the court process. The workers also convey information to the crown attorney when victims request variations in bail conditions and/or indicate that they want to
have the Crown stay proceedings. A third component involves desig-
nating special courtrooms for first appearances, with screening courts
and trials, to expedite processing of domestic violence cases. Initially,
fourteen designated judges sat in these courtrooms, but as the volume
rapidly increased, all provincial court judges now rotate through the
designated courts.

One of the consequences of this specialization was a redefinition of the "work culture" in the FVC prosecution unit. Prior to specialization, neither the structure nor values of the crown attorney's office were responsive to the needs of domestic violence victims. For prosecutors, the traditional definition of success was conviction. In this environment "domestics" had been low-profile, difficult cases with minimal chances for conviction. Structurally, the conviction standard of success punished crown attorneys who invested time in domestic cases.

The creation of the specialized family violence unit in prosecutions was a necessary but not sufficient impetus to change the prosecutorial culture. The critical complement to the structural changes was the introduction of policy guidelines to assist crown attorneys in the prosecution of domestic violence cases. These guidelines reflect the dual consideration of rigorous prosecution and sensitivity to the victim. This policy opened the door to questioning the traditional objectives of prosecution. Previously, the only way to get a conviction was to subpoena the witness and, in some cases, treat her as a "hostile witness," clearly revictimizing the victim. The dual mandate of rigorous prosecution and sensitivity to the needs of the victim has the potential to encompass a wider array of objectives, including victim safety, communicating to the offender the unacceptability of violence, and potentially investing victims with greater power and agency in dealing with a violent partner (Worden, 2000). Each of these outcomes can be achieved in the absence of a conviction. While the dual mandate set a high standard of performance for the crown attorney that exceeds the single measure of conviction, it also extends a broad range of discretion to achieve that standard. It bears no resemblance to the no-drop policy. In identifying the victim as a priority equal in importance to the goals of rigorous prosecution, the guidelines direct crown attorneys to consider the needs of the victim as their reference point in exercising their discretion.

Some might consider this dual mandate as unworkable. With specialization, however, this has not been the case. It does require crown prosecutors to tolerate a high stay rate, with the knowledge, however, that victims who are not able or willing to testify at one point in time may well do so after they have exhausted all other alternatives. Crown attorneys have rich anecdotal evidence about women who decided to testify after numerous unsuccessful attempts to control their partner's behaviour through police calls alone. This parallels the experiences of shelter workers who report that women frequently use shelter services a number of times, returning to their abusive partner each time with the hope that the abuse will end (MacLeod, 1987; 1989). In this context, stays of proceedings should be understood as part of a long process in which women pursue many remedies short of a final break—i.e., divorce or testimony to convict—to secure their safety (MacLeod, 1987; Ford and Burke, 1987; Snyder and Scheer, 1981). It is, fundamentally important that in this process women do not receive the message that failure to "cooperate fully with the prosecutor" at one point in time implies forfeiting her right to legal intervention in the future. For this reason, it is critical for the crown attorneys to understand their role in terms of "process."

In Winnipeg, over time, the culture of the prosecution's office has changed. Crown attorneys have been able to let go of the one-dimensional "conviction" measure of success and adopt a process perspective, assisting victims in securing a safer life. In this light, "justice" becomes less about "Crown success in court" and more about the victim/family's need to redress a destructive power imbalance. This new reference point results in much greater consideration of the victim's pragmatic interests that, in turn, shapes the crown attorney's behaviour and court outcomes. Two distinctive outcomes of the guidelines for prosecution of domestic violence cases are the introduction of testimony bargaining and Crown acceptance of higher stay rates.

In the Winnipeg FVC, the most frequent outcome of an arrest for domestic assault is a stay of proceedings (46 percent) and the second most frequent outcome is a guilty plea (43 percent). The crown attorneys play a critical role in both outcomes. The zero tolerance policy provides for a wide catchment of cases at the front end of the system and prosecutorial discretion results in a funneling of cases through the system. Stays of proceedings and guilty pleas are an important part of the funneling process. Stays of proceedings occur when there is no reasonable chance of conviction and, therefore, no reasonable grounds for proceeding to court. Guilty pleas reduce court time by limiting the court's role to the determination of sentences.

When determining whether to stay a case or to proceed, the evidence is paramount. As discussed earlier, a characteristic of domestic violence cases that typically occur behind closed doors is that evidence often depends on whether the victim is willing to testify. Thus, before considering stay rates and the various concerns they raise, we will examine several of the Crown's strategies to increase the victim's willingness to testify. These strategies impact guilty pleas and, consequently, reduce the number of stays of proceedings.

Plea Bargaining and Testimony Bargaining

Plea bargaining is one of the least visible, most extensive and most controversial practices of crown attorneys (Genova, 1981; Verdun-Jones and Hatch, 1985). The Law Reform Commission of Canada (1975, p. 45) defines a plea bargain as "any agreement by the accused to plead guilty in return for the promise of some benefit." Typically, plea bargaining is understood as the process whereby the crown attorney agrees to proceed on lesser or fewer charges in order to obtain a guilty plea.

There is no formal policy on plea bargaining in the FVC or any other court (it is practised extensively in the FVC). Canadian studies suggest that plea bargaining occurs in 60 to 70 percent of criminal cases (Solomon, 1983; Ericson and Baranek, 1982). Eighty percent of the cases that proceed to court in FVC are the result of a guilty plea. About 70 percent of the guilty pleas in FVC are entered in docket or screening court (Ursel, 1995). In these early plea bargain cases, the "bargain" is typically between the crown attorney and the defence and/or accused. However, another form of bargaining occurs in FVC, which may be unique to this specialized court. In such cases, the crown attorney "bargains" with the victim/witness. These examples of "testimony bargaining" typically occur when cases are scheduled for trial, and the victim is reluctant to testify because of her fear that her partner will go to jail. The crown attorney will discuss the case with the reluctant witness and indicate a willingness to reduce the number or severity of the charges, and/or recommend probation and court-mandated treatment in return for the victim/witness's cooperation. Guilty pleas entered at trial, when the accused and defence counsel observe the presence of the witness, are often a result of "testimony bargaining."

The characteristic feature of family violence cases, victim dependence on and bonding with the accused, is probably the single most important factor in explaining the high rate of plea bargaining and the unusual practice of testimony bargaining found in FVC. Successful plea bargaining meets the requirements of rigorous prosecution and achieves court intervention and sentencing while sparing the victim the trauma of testifying. The crown attorney's ability to obtain a sentence is greatly reduced if the case goes to trial. Through the process of traditional plea bargaining, or the more innovative testimony bargaining, the crown attorney is able to meet the dual and potentially conflicting mandates of rigorous prosecution and sensitivity to the victim.

Stays of Proceedings

Despite hard work by crown attorneys to achieve a guilty plea, the strategy does not always work. The stay rate in family violence court over the five years reviewed is 46 percent. This would be discouraging if conviction was the only measure of success. This rate reflects, in part, the prosecutor's unwillingness to "prosecute at all costs." The dual mandate with which the prosecutors work reminds them not to revictimize the victim through forcing a prosecution that she does not want or for which she is not ready to serve as a witness. As a result, a number of cases will not proceed due to the victim's expressed needs and interests or her failure to appear at the trial.

However, in examining the stay rate it is important to note that court statistics reflect the "single-incident" framework of the CJS. We measure cases as they come into the system and are disposed. They are a snap shot in time. This can have the effect of overestimating the stay rate in the long term. For example, if we refer back to the Ash case, Mr. Ash shows up in our statistics five times over eleven years, constituting four stays of proceedings despite the fact that the 1998 arrest resulted in Mr. Ash being prosecuted and convicted on the charges accumulated from all of the arrests. Anecdotal information from the prosecutors suggests that the Ash case is not an isolated incident.

The crown attorneys in Winnipeg have come to appreciate the repetitive and cyclic nature of family violence and understand that women who are unwilling or unable to testify at one point in time may well cooperate with the Crown and provide strong evidence in the future. Thus it is important that the Crown leave the message with the victim that she will not be harassed with warrants for failing to appear, and she will not be treated as a hostile witness if she recants. It is important that the victim knows that the system is there to help her, and she will be taken seriously and treated with respect if charges are laid in the future.

The Ash case is particularly instructive in understanding why women are often unable or unwilling to testify. As noted previously, the case against Mr. Ash was stayed four times due to Mrs. Ash's failure to appear at the trial. What the court learned during the final trial was that, in each case, Mrs. Ash was sent out of province to stay with family and friends of Mr. Ash while he kept the children at home. In the final trial, Mr. Ash was additionally charged with four counts of obstructing justice for these acts that had prevented Mrs. Ash from testifying in the earlier trials.

Court Processing and Outcome

Despite the considerable challenges that crown attorneys face in prosecuting domestic violence cases, 54 percent of FVC cases proceeded to court. Of the spouse abuse cases, 85 percent of the accused were men and 85 percent of the victims were women. The majority, 73 percent of the cases, involved ongoing relationships, with 36 percent common-law, 18 percent married and 19 percent boyfriend-girlfriend. Estranged relationships accounted for 24 percent of the cases that came to court.

The most frequent charge was common assault: 85 percent of the cases involved a physical assault of varying degrees of severity from common assault to murder. Breaches of court orders or probation orders in the absence of any other charge constituted 13 percent of the cases, sexual assault charges accounted for 2 percent and criminal harassment, 1 percent of all cases. Many of the accused may have been arrested with numerous charges, although if they pled guilty they were likely to have been sentenced on fewer charges.

There are two different types of incidents in the FVC data, those in which the spouse alone was the victim, and multiple victim cases, like the Ash case, in which spouse and children were abused. Because we are discussing the larger data set in relation to the Ash case, we thought it would be interesting to compare the court processing of the spouse-alone cases to the spouse-and-child abuse cases. Our data indicate differences in the outcome of these cases at all stages of the court process.

Table 3-1
Court Processing of Cases by Type of Abuse
Winnipeg FVC 1992/93–1997/98

Case Status	Spouse (alone) N = 13,868		Spouse/Child N = 339	
	Number	Percentage	Number	Percentage
Stayed	6,410	46	87	26
Guilty Pleas	5,971	43	206	61

At the first stage of court processing, the determination of stays of proceedings and the entry of guilty pleas, there are substantial differences in the two types of case resulting in a higher conviction rate for spouse/child cases. These differences may be the result of a number of factors. Child abuse cases generally have a higher conviction rate than spouse abuse cases. Crown attorneys may be much more reluctant to stay a case involving child victims as indicated by the substantially lower stay rate for spouse/child cases than spouse alone cases. Second, women are often motivated to take action when their child(ren) has/have been hurt, including showing a greater willingness to testify. Finally, depending on the age of the child, these cases may also have multiple witnesses, thus the crown attorney is not solely dependent on the spouse's attitude about testifying. The greater likelihood of testimony by the victim/witnesses in spouse/child abuse cases accounts for the dramatic difference in rates of dismissed for want of prosecution (DFWOP) indicated in Table 3-2 on trial outcomes.

Table 3-2
Trial Outcomes by Type of Abuse
Winnipeg FVC 1992/93–1997/98

| | Spouse (alone) N = 1,494 | | Spouse/Child N = 39 | |
	Number	Percentage	Number	Percentage
DFWOP	750	50	14	36
Guilty Verdict	431	29	19	49
Not Guilty	297	20	6	15

Because of the lower DFWOP rate of spouse/child abuse cases, more proceed through a complete trial, resulting in a much higher rate of guilty verdicts. When we add together the guilty pleas with the guilty verdicts, spouse/child abuse cases have a much higher conviction rate, 66 percent compared to 46 percent for spouse-alone cases.

Sentencing

Prior to specialization within the Winnipeg criminal justice system, the most frequent outcome for a convicted spouse abuse offender was a conditional discharge (Ursel, 1992). This meant no treatment, no punishment, no record of criminal behaviour—in short, no consequences. Women's advocates, in particular, were concerned about the lack of serious consequences for spouse abusers. This concern, in combination with the increasing number of family violence matters coming to court, led to the development of the Family Violence Court. Since the implementation of FVC in 1990, sentencing practices have changed dramatically.

The most frequent sentence for spouse and spouse/child abuse offenders is supervised probation and court-mandated treatment; the second most frequent outcome is incarceration (See Table 3-3). As in all criminal courts, offenders often receive multiple sentences because they usually have multiple charges. The Winnipeg FVC is no exception.

Table 3-3
Sentencing by Type of Abuse
Winnipeg FVC 1992/93–1997/98

	Spouse	Spouse and Child
Total Convicted	6,402	225
	Percentage	Percentage
Probation	70	81
Incarceration	22*	36
Fine	17	13

*When we add time in custody at sentence, the number of offenders who were incarcerated rises to 35%. Time in custody figures for Spouse/Child are not available at this point.

While the general sentencing pattern remains the same for the two types of cases, there is a marked tendency for spouse/child cases to have more serious outcomes, including higher probation rates, higher incarceration rates and a lower proportion of fines. This tendency is also evident in comparisons of the length of incarceration by type of abuse as indicated in Table 3-4.

Table 3-4
Length of Incarceration by Type of Abuse
Winnipeg FVC 1992/93–1997/98

	Spouse	Spouse and Child
Total Convicted	1,376	81
	Percentage	Percentage
3 months or less	72	53
4–11 months	24	38
1 year or more	4	9

At the beginning of this chapter I remarked that the twenty-five-year sentence for Mr. Ash was most unusual. The majority of the sentences for spouse abuse cases are seldom longer than a few months. However, it is significant to note that in comparing the two types of cases, spouse/child cases are given longer sentences than the spouse-alone cases. Only a few cases in each type of abuse received sentences of years rather than months. In the spouse-alone category three offenders received five-year sentences, two received six-year sentences and one offender was sentenced to eight and a half years. The lengthiest sentence in our five years of data was sixteen years. Within the spouse/child category, one offender was sentenced to one and a half years; the longest sentence was seven years.

Conclusion

I end the chapter as I began, remarking on the unusual sentence for Mr. Ash, relative to the 14,207 cases reviewed above. His extraordinary sentence reflects the extreme brutality of his offences. We are not suggesting that all offenders should receive lengthy jail sentences, and we do applaud the court's attention to rehabilitation as evidenced in the high number of cases mandated to treatment. However, the Ash case does provide a dramatic example of the difficulties involved in "doing justice" in domestic violence cases. We believe that the remarkable perseverance of the police, the crown attorneys and the judges over the twelve years of arrests, interventions and setbacks, demonstrates a growing awareness of the "process nature" of these cases and a willingness to accommodate this process.

As I write this chapter in mid-July of 2001, Mr. Ash's defence lawyer has filed for an appeal. It will be most interesting to see how this request is handled, for although the Ash case is extraordinary in many regards, it is also typical in terms of life patterns and abuse history. Thus, the outcome of this appeal will be of interest to advocates for women and children as a most dramatic example of how our justice system deals with the abuse of vulnerable family members.

What both the Ash case and the 14,207 cases reviewed above reveal, is that many women and children are much in need of protection, and our criminal justice system must play an important role in securing that protection. In the victim impact statement read to the court when Mr. Ash was sentenced, Mrs. Ash stated that her husband's sentence was her own because he had many times threatened revenge. His twenty-five years in jail would be her twenty-five years of freedom.

Notes

1. We have changed the name of the family out of respect for their right to privacy.
2. A stay of proceedings is probably the legal equivalent of "limbo": since there is no finding of guilt and there is no determination of innocence, the case simply does not proceed through the court because of a lack of evidence. This is very typical of many wife abuse cases when the victim is unwilling or unable to testify.
3. The Winnipeg FVC data presented in this chapter cover a five-year period, 1992/93 to 1997/98. The data are collected from all incoming domestic violence matters in which an arrest was made. This represents a complete population of family violence cases rather than a sample. The only missing cases are those in which the accused died before disposition or is out on warrant and the case is not disposed. Cases are considered family violence matters if the victim is in a relationship with the accused which involves "trust, dependency and/or kinship." Thus, the FVC hears matters of child abuse, spouse abuse, elder abuse and other family assaults, including abuse between adult siblings, nieces, nephews, uncles and aunts. While the court adjudicates four types of interpersonal abuse, our discussion in this chapter will be limited to spousal abuse cases. Therefore, our analysis will focus on the 14,207 spouse abuse matters heard over the five years under review. Included in this total are 339 cases involving abuse of both the spouse and child/ren. Within our data set, spouse abuse includes all cases of adult intimate relations in which the victim is between the ages of eighteen and fifty-nine years of age. Victims under the age of eighteen fall into the realm of child abuse, and victims sixty years and over fall into the elder abuse category, even though, in both cases it could be an intimate partner abusing them. It is interesting to note that, despite this conservative definition of spouse abuse, these cases constitute 85 percent of the matters before FVC. Our unit of analysis is the individual and not the charge, because while many individuals enter the system with multiple charges, they may be sentenced on only one or two of these.
4. Components of the policy changes apply throughout the province of Manitoba, but in some of the smaller communities the lower volume of cases do not permit specialization at the court level.
5. The 1999–2000 Transition Home Survey is conducted on a biennial basis as part of the federal government's Family Violence Initiative. The questionnaire was sent to 508 shelters in Canada known to be providing residential services for women victims and their children. Responses were received from 467 shelters (92 percent). Women in shelters were asked if they had called the police in the most recent violence incident they had experienced and whether the police had laid a charge.
6. Not all of the calls listed as domestic involve a crime. Often neighbours will call about a loud argument. On average police do lay a charge in approximately one third of calls that are identified as domestic.

Chapter Four

Leave Him or Lose Them?
The Child Protection Response to Woman Abuse
Kendra Nixon[1]

Although women are most frequently the direct victims of intimate violence, there is growing evidence that children exposed to violence perpetrated against their mothers may also be affected, sometimes seriously. Child welfare professionals in Canada have recently acknowledged the detrimental effects on children of witnessing violence. To date, six Canadian provinces have included specific clauses in their child protection legislation that address exposure to violence within the home. Battered women's advocates have criticized these amendments as failing to protect children, further victimizing abused women and ignoring abusive men. This chapter discusses the debate about child welfare intervention in cases of woman abuse through examining the responses of eight front-line child protection workers in one Canadian child welfare authority.

The Effects on Children Exposed to Woman Abuse
A number of researchers have concluded that witnessing abuse can be damaging to a child's cognitive, emotional, social, developmental and physical well-being (Carroll, 1994; Dawson, 1990; Hershorn and Rosenbaum, 1985; Hughes and Hampton, 1984; Jaffe, Wolfe and Wilson, 1990; Moore, Pepler, Mae and Kates, 1989; Straus and Gelles, 1996; Sudermann, 1997). Children who witness woman abuse often exhibit symptoms similar to children who themselves have been physically, sexually and/or emotionally abused (Hershorn and Rosenbaum, 1985; Jaffe et al., 1990). Exposure to woman abuse may be related to internalizing problems such as depression, low self-esteem and withdrawal, as well as externalizing problems including rebellion, hyperactivity and delinquency (Dawson, 1990; Jaffe et al., 1990; Moore et al., 1989). In addition, male children who witness woman abuse may be at an in-

creased risk of becoming perpetrators (Hughes and Hampton, 1984; Jaffe et al., 1990).

In addition to the effects on children of witnessing abuse, there is evidence of a significant overlap between woman abuse and child physical abuse (Edleson, 1999; Farmer and Owen, 1995; Straus and Gelles, 1996). Straus and Gelles (1996) found that 50 percent of the men who assaulted their wives also assaulted their children. Hughes (1988) concluded that children who have been physically abused in addition to witnessing abuse exhibit the most serious negative effects.

Nevertheless, almost all of the studies documenting the harmful effects on children who witnessed abuse also found children who were not affected (Hughes and Barad, 1983; Hughes and Luke, 1998; Jaffe et al., 1990; Rosenbaum and O'Leary, 1981). Kolbo (1996) notes that some children are resilient and may be protected because of factors such as external support systems, affectionate family ties, communication skills and individual coping skills (see also Magen, 1999).

Thus there may be a correlation between witnessing woman abuse and children's negative behavioural and emotional responses—but this is not necessarily a causative relationship. Witnessing woman abuse may be merely one of the negative events in a child's life, nor is it likely the only type of violence witnessed. Magen (1999) reminds us that many children are exposed to media violence and violence in their community. Children whose parents are involved in a highly contested divorce may experience negative reactions similar to those of children who witness woman abuse, yet they are not subject to the same child welfare scrutiny. It is likely impossible to accurately assess all of the different types of violence and aggression that a child may experience. Therefore, although it is important that we recognize the possible detrimental effects of witnessing violence on children, it is equally critical to acknowledge that not all children are similarly affected and that children's resilience and ability to survive should not be underestimated (Humphreys, 1997).

Child Protection and Woman Abuse

The increased attention to children exposed to violence within the home has resulted in some provincial child welfare authorities classifying this exposure as a form of child maltreatment and subsequently amending their legislation. This not only allows child protection workers to intervene when woman abuse is identified, it also allows them to possibly apprehend children. Such legislative changes have been implemented with little forethought or discussion as to their potential impact on child welfare practice and, ultimately, on abused women and their children.

Although the goal of social policy is to improve the welfare of citizens, some social policies introduced with the best intentions may, in fact, have the opposite effect. Child protection legislation that mandates intervention when "domestic violence" is identified has been severely criticized as further victimizing abused women, ignoring male perpetrators, and ultimately, not protecting children.

One concern is that the legislative amendments use gender-neutral terminology when describing what is primarily violence against female intimate partners (Echlin and Marshall, 1994). For example, Alberta's legislation uses terms such as "domestic violence" and "domestic disharmony" to characterize violence occurring within the home. Battered women's advocates have argued that such wording distorts the reality of the situation—that the victims are almost always women and children. Gender-neutral language also fails to attribute any accountability and responsibility for the abuse to the male batterer and minimizes the abuse perpetrated against the mother.

Such legislative change has also been strongly criticized because it allows a child to be apprehended if the woman's abuse is discovered (Law Reform Commission of Nova Scotia, 1995). Fearing the apprehension of her children, an abused woman will likely not disclose her abuse and will remain in an abusive situation (National Council of Juvenile and Family Court Judges Family Violence Department, 1999; Whitney and Davis, 1999). Further, given that such legislative amendments will include mandatory reporting, shelter workers are concerned that they will be mandated to report abused women and their children to child protective services. Shelter workers may be viewed as "agents" of the state rather than allies or advocates for abused women, which will, no doubt, irrevocably damage the relationship between shelters and abused women (Echlin and Marshall, 1994).

Including woman abuse in child protection legislation has also been considered problematic because attention is almost always focused on the abused mother (Beeman and Edleson, 2000; Callahan, 1993; Carter and Schechter, 1997; Farmer and Owen, 1995; Humphreys, 1999; Humphreys, 1997; Hutchison, 1992; Krane, 1997; Magen, 1999; Miccio, 1995; Milner, 1993; Schechter and Edleson, 1995; Whitney and Davis, 1999). Hutchison (1992) suggests that a gender bias exists in the child welfare system which holds women to different standards than men. In the case of woman abuse, women are held responsible for the abuse and must alleviate the abusive situation. Child welfare efforts tend to exclusively focus on battered women's ability to protect their children, while the men who commit the violence are largely ignored. Mothers and fathers are often subjected to markedly different investigative and intervention approaches (Milner, 1993). For example, because mothers are seen as responsible for the care of their children, when something goes wrong, the mother is blamed for inadequacy and negligence. On the other hand, abusive men are frequently invisible in the child welfare system (Beeman, Hagemeister and Edleson, 1999; Callahan, 1993; Edleson, 1999; Edleson, 1998; Farmer and Owen, 1995; Humphreys, 1999; Humphreys, 1997; Krane, 1997; Magen, 1999; Miccio, 1995; Milner, 1993; Mullender, 1996; Peled, 1993; Stanley, 1997; Swift, 1998). If the father's abusive behaviour is mentioned in child welfare practice it is usually only viewed in the context of what the mother failed to prevent (Miccio, 1995). Fathers not only disappear from the system, but they are frequently and deliberately excluded (Milner, 1993). Stanley (1997) argues that "without a social work focus on men that involves exposing and examining their violence, mothers in situations of domestic violence may be left carrying intolerable burdens, and child protection intervention may prove at worst, oppressive, or at best, ineffective" (1997, p. 143).

When women remain in abusive situations they are often considered by child welfare systems as "failing to protect" their children because they do not stop the abuse (Beeman and Edleson, 2000; Beeman, Hagemeister and Edleson, 1999; Carter and Schechter, 1997; Echlin and Osthoff, 2000; Edleson and Beeman, 2000; Magen, 1999; Miccio, 1995; Milner, 1993). This suggests that the failure is due to the battered woman not taking the "appropriate" action (i.e., leaving the abusive situation) to protect her children. Further, abused women are often perceived by child welfare systems as inadequate parents who cannot care for the physical and emotional well-being of their children. For instance, in their experience with child protection workers, Whitney and Davis found that "team discussions about mothers often turned quickly to what the worker viewed as the woman's pathology, her participation in her abuse, her lack of concern for protecting her children, her repeated choice of abusive partners, and so on" (1999, p. 159). Similarly, Peled (1993) concluded that abused mothers are frequently accused of failing to protect their children by having relationships with abusive men.

Abused women are often perceived as emotionally unavailable to their children, aggressive, lacking appropriate discipline skills and having impaired parenting capabilities (Aron and Olson, 1997). However, a growing body of literature casts serious doubts on the assumption that battered women are helpless, inadequate and incompetent parents (Levendosky, Lynch, and Graham-Bermann, 2000; Schechter and Edleson, 1994; Sullivan, Nguyen, Allen, Bybee, and Juras, 2000). Sullivan et al. (2000) found no evidence that abused women are inadequate or aggressive parents. In fact, the majority of mothers who participated in the study agreed that they were available to their children, closely supervised them and enjoyed being parents. The study also found no evidence to support the common perception that battered women experience greater parenting stress and use more inappropriate discipline than non-battered women.

Another study about mothers' perceptions of the impact of abuse reported not only negative effects on their parenting but also some positive effects (Levendosky et al., 2000): abused women frequently and actively mobilize their resources to respond to the violence on behalf of their children. Schechter and Edleson (1995) also concluded that many abused women take active steps to protect their children despite the unpredictability of the violence and the effects of the violence on them. Often, little attention is paid to the woman's actions that protect her children, ones that must be taken into consideration when evaluating her parenting ability ("Failure to Protect" Working Group, 2000). Further, Haddix (1996) asserts that, once freed from an abusive relationship, abused women frequently regain coping skills, establish normal lives and improve the lives of their children.

Systems that blame women for remaining in violent situations and attribute the problem to their individual "inadequacies" often pay little attention to women's socio-economic realities. Child welfare policy and practice, in general, often fail to recognize that many women remain in abusive relationships because they are financially dependent on their male partners (Callahan, 1993; Swift, 1998). In fact, many women are no safer and much poorer when they leave violent partners. Women often stay in violent relationships because of their inability to support themselves and their children independently (Callahan, 1993). Unfortunately, the child protection system rarely makes this connection.

The overlap between woman abuse and child maltreatment should indicate to child protection professionals that the abuser must be held accountable and that intervention must include him. Because of the high rate of recidivism among batterers, when they form new relationships any new offspring may also witness violence (Haddix, 1996). Therefore, if child welfare considers it important to intervene in cases of woman abuse, it must intervene and hold abusive fathers responsible, instead of narrowly focusing their efforts solely on abused women.

Some authors have acknowledged the detrimental impact of child welfare intervention on women and children when intimate partner abuse is identified (Armitage, 1993; Callahan, 1993; Mullender, 1996; Parkinson and Humphreys, 1998; "Failure to Protect" Working Group, 2000). Children exposed to marital violence are at high risk of being apprehended, especially if such exposure is enshrined in child protection legislation (Farmer and Owen, 1995; Humphreys, 1997; "Failure to Protect" Working Group, 2000). Humphreys (1997) discovered in her sample of thirty-two families where domestic violence was identified, that 50 percent of families had children who were apprehended by local child welfare authorities when woman abuse was identified.

Removing children from the non-abusive mother often has severe and long-lasting effects on children ("Failure to Protect" Working Group, 2000). Children who witness violence against their mothers are already victimized by fear and feelings of helplessness. They often struggle with anger, grief, anxiety and feelings of being responsible for the abuse. Removing them from their mothers re-victimizes them, compounding their distress by increasing fears of abandonment. Armitage (1993) also suggests that if a child is apprehended, adjustment difficulties may be created or already-present problems exacerbated. Research in the areas of separation and loss reveals that separating a child from her/his family can be tremendously emotionally damaging. Authors such as Callahan (1993) clearly link the status of women and the well-being of children: the more disadvantaged the mother, the more disadvantaged the child. Generally, the best way to protect children is to protect and empower their mothers (Aron and Olson, 1997; Farmer and Owen, 1995; Findlater and Kelly, 1999; Hutchison, 1992; Miller, 1987).

The Responses of Child Protection Workers: A Canadian Study

The *Child Welfare Act* of Alberta mandates that children are in need of protection if they suffer emotional injury as the result of exposure to "domestic violence" or "severe domestic disharmony," and the guardian fails to protect them. I conducted the following research to discover how front-line child protection workers in Alberta handle cases of woman abuse and how the legislation impacts on the way in which they intervene in such cases. The remainder of the chapter highlights the research results and provides insights into the heated debate of whether or not child protection authorities should be intervening in cases of woman abuse.

Eight front-line child protection workers from an Alberta child welfare authority were interviewed and participated in a follow-up focus group. The participants were selected because of their direct client experience in the area of child protection. In terms of their demographics, six of the eight participants were Caucasian, and two identified as Aboriginal. Seven of the eight workers were female. The length of the participants' child welfare experience varied. One had ten years background in child welfare, five had worked for from two to five years, and two had worked less than two years. Four respondents have B.S.W. degrees; three have M.S.W. degrees; and one has an undergraduate degree in criminology. Six workers reported prior experience working with abused women; six had additional training in domestic violence; and five had participated in child welfare training programs. Finally, in terms of personal experiences, three workers had been victims of intimate partner violence themselves, and one respondent grew up in a household where domestic violence had occurred.

Gender-Neutral View of Woman Abuse

All of the workers readily acknowledged that woman abuse is a serious problem within child welfare practice and that witnessing violence has a significant negative impact on children. However, most construed this violence as "fighting" or "marital conflict." Despite our extensive knowledge that perpetrators are almost always male and victims are almost always female, the workers conceptualized the problem as gender-neutral, with the abusive behaviour occurring *between* the two partners. Consider the following comments:

> You need to say to this family, "your fighting could cause you to lose your children."

> The police have been out a couple of times, and clearly the statements say that the child is being held while they [the spouses] are fighting. So there is a risk of physical harm—it's domestic violence, this mother is being beat up.

> It's pretty much part of my standard interview with the child— to find out what Mom and Dad do when they are mad at each other. Do they hit each other?

Even when the workers clearly identified the man as the abuser, they perceived both parents as mutually engaging in the abusive behaviour. Workers rarely conceptualized the problem as male violence towards the female partner, even though they provided countless examples of the male partner perpetrating violence towards his female partner.

The gender-neutral view of the problem may be attributed, in part, to the gender-neutral terminology used in Alberta's child welfare legislation, which identifies woman abuse as "domestic violence" or "domestic disharmony." Since social policies are framed according to how social problems are defined, violence against intimate female partners has been defined as gender-neutral and has been enshrined as such in the legislation.

Given the workers' conceptualization of the problem, it is not surprising that their interventions did not concentrate on the man's violence towards the woman. Instead, the interventions often focused on alleviating the violence "between" the partners, mainly through mandating the parents to counselling:

> If they both acknowledge that it is going on, I usually talk to both of them and make a determination that they are going to get into some counselling. If it is severe enough, I would go to

court and I would seek a supervision order so that I can ensure that they will do the counselling ... but all the courses in the world aren't going to help if the two people don't want to change their behaviour.

If they don't follow through with anything on that [supervision order] ... the child can be apprehended real quickly.

The parents are not being responsible—they are not doing anything about it.

Even in situations in which the male partner was the obvious perpetrator, the woman was considered responsible for alleviating the problem. As one worker commented:

Dad punched Mom, she had bruises, [and] she went to the hospital. They plan to go to counselling and I want a supervision order to ensure they attend counselling.

The Abused Woman as the Focus of Intervention

The concern raised in the literature that abused women are frequently the focus of child welfare efforts was confirmed in the present study. The child welfare workers primarily focused their interventions on the abused woman, insisting that she is responsible for alleviating the problem.

Then you need to be saying to the parents or to the wife, specifically (this is the majority who you say it to), "You need to make a decision, you're going to either keep exposing your children to this kind of behaviour, or we may take a more intrusive role which could be removing the children from the home."

They [women] are seen as the primary guardian and as the guardian they have—they should have—they need to protect. There is more onus on them to protect than there is the [male] partner."

I've had a family with continuing family violence issues and I said to her, "You're going to have to make a choice here between protecting your children and being with this man."

There appears to be a gender bias within the child welfare system (Callahan, 1993; Gordon, 1988; Hutchison, 1992; Miller, 1987). Women, today, are still held responsible for the well-being of the family members: the unequal ways in which parenting roles are played out are never more clearly seen than in the families served by the child welfare system (Costin, 1985, p. 201). Because women are viewed as responsible for the care and control of their children, they are blamed for being inadequate and negligent when something happens to children (Milner, 1993, p. 52). Historically, mother-blaming was a prominent phenomenon, so that when neglect and/or abuse was identified, women were deemed responsible because they were in charge of children's care (Gordon, 1988). This is no different today. The practice of mother-blaming is clearly evident in the responses of the child protection workers.

The workers appeared to place strong expectations on abused women to follow through with the case plan. If not, the women could expect more intrusive measures, including the removal of their children. In one startling example, even when a woman made efforts (presumably set out in the case plan) to seek help, she was punished:

> The father of her four youngest ones wasn't living at home but he would come around and visit. And I would say, "You know, I don't have a problem with that as long as he's not coming around and demanding things of you and not abusing [you] verbally, especially in front of the kids." And so that was fine.... We were visiting Mom on a regular basis, every month [as] she had a supervision order. She went to [domestic violence counselling program]. She was having another baby. She had her own place and I guess he came there one weekend and got on her case about something. I think it had something to do with the service plan. He got mad and kicked her in the stomach. She phoned the police. He left. They [the police] put it down as a complaint. And I confronted her, "Where were these kids when he kicked you?" She said they were sleeping. I said, "I don't think they were sleeping. This is not right. If you want to continue the relationship with so and so, then we'll be more intrusive with you and your family."

It appears that this woman did everything that an abused woman "should do"—she lived apart from her abusive ex-partner, she attended counselling and she called the police when her ex-partner assaulted her. Still, child welfare focused their efforts on her. Ultimately, she was held responsible for the abuse when, in fact, others should have been: her ex-partner for abusing her, the police for not laying charges or arresting the perpetrator, and child welfare also for not intervening with the perpetrator. Furthermore, the child welfare worker speculated that the woman's ex-partner became angry and physically abusive when he found out about the child welfare service plan. If this is the case, are child welfare workers aware of the potential dangers of their interventions on abused women?

In a similar case, an abused woman was the focus of child welfare intervention, and her children were subsequently apprehended:

> There was some speculation that Mom had gotten beaten up by her new relationship. But I found out she got beaten up by an ex-boyfriend, the brother of this new relationship. But the kids were around—the kids were apprehended. Mom was taken to the hospital. So there was this really big mix-up, [we] thought it was domestic abuse, but it was somebody else—not her new relationship.

In this situation, even when the woman had left the abusive relationship, she was still held accountable for the abuse perpetrated against her.

The child welfare workers indicated that one common expectation of abused women is that they separate from or remain separated from men who are violent:

> I think if it is severe domestic violence, most child welfare workers would be saying to the wife, "You need to be making a decision, you stay with your husband or you leave your husband and take your children to a safe place until your family gets involved in therapy and does some of the work, and some anger management skills are learned or we remove your children."

> If it's [the abuse] a second time incident we usually go to court on a supervision order. We would just walk into the family with the order in hand and say, "Obviously things didn't go as well as planned." I think it's made, at least I make it clear, that if I'm going out for a second time, then if it happens a third time, the kids are gone. Whether it's Mom moves out with the kids, or we remove the kids.

It is naive and dangerous to believe that abused women and their children will be made safer by leaving abusive partners. It is well known that after leaving abusive relationships women are often at higher risk of injury (Fleury, Sullivan and Bybee, 2000; Magen, 1999; Mahoney, 1991). Women may be stalked, harassed, assaulted and sometimes killed after separating from an abusive partner.

Furthermore, assuming that the abused mother should separate from the abusive partner implies that stopping the abuse is her responsibility. As one worker posed the question, "If it's that bad, why doesn't she just leave?" This thinking also implies that the abused woman has the responsibility to achieve separation and that she *can* separate. Not only is this problematic because it puts the focus on the woman's behaviour, but it also assumes both that leaving is a viable solution to the abuse and that leaving is appropriate and an option for all women. Available and affordable housing does not always exist and emergency shelters are often full. Even if shelter space is available, transition houses are rarely able to meet all of the abused woman's needs (e.g., financial support, employment, housing, child care); they do so for only a brief period of time.

The workers did not indicate why they believed that separating from the abusive partner was an appropriate expectation. Perhaps they have not received adequate training and so do not realize that this expectation is not always available or feasible for many abused women. Perhaps insisting that abused women separate from their abusers is the only intervention available to workers. They may believe that they have no other recourse to protect children.

The context in which these workers practice often makes it difficult to provide the necessary services, especially when child welfare systems tend to be understaffed, lack resources to respond adequately to the needs of those receiving services and are primarily crisis-driven (Wharf and McKenzie, 1998). Consequently, child protection workers are often not able to provide the support and services that are most needed by abused women and their children, such as housing or economic assistance.

The Abused Woman's Inadequacy

Similar to the current literature, the responses of the workers often involved statements about the abused woman's inadequacies—her lack of parenting skills, her "inability" to protect her children, her "unwillingness" to protect her children, her lack of awareness or knowledge of the impact the abuse has on her children and/or her inability to choose non-abusive partners:

> But when you first get involved, she may not have that ability [to protect her children from the abuse], so you may have to take more intrusive steps to protect the child so she learns those skills.

> Success for Mom might be that she is able to protect the children more appropriately.

They just don't have the knowledge of how [violence impacts on children].

Sometimes you can give them [abused women] all the services you want, but they don't learn. They are not going to attach to the services and actually follow through in learning.

[The] situation right now is very frustrating … because Mom can leave this man but is already in the bed of another man.

If they don't [receive] therapy, they will pick another abusive spouse. If you don't learn, you are going to pick the same kind of partner. So I think if you leave an abusive partner, I don't think child welfare should walk away. I think we should work with the woman when they're away from their husband or abusive male. I think we should start doing work on their self-esteem and to teach them how to recognize these kinds of guys and how to work through some of these issues so they don't pick the same kind of man, because they do. They pick the same kind of man over and over and over again. They don't know any better.

The preceding research review contradicted the worker's assumptions. Abused women are, on average, no different in their parenting ability than non-abused women. They are often competent and affectionate parents who take active steps to protect their children. Many abused women clearly recognize the effects of violence on their children. In terms of "choosing" abusive partners, research has failed to conclude that unless abused women receive therapy, they will continue to choose abusive partners.

Perhaps the workers' attention on abused women's inadequacies is an effect of the language contained in Alberta's child protection legislation. For example, the legislation uses such value-laden words as "unable" and "unwilling" to describe a parent who is not protecting the child. This language implies that the guardian is somehow inadequate or deficient and therefore, cannot properly care for her children. Historically, child welfare efforts have tended to focus on the individual inadequacies and shortcomings of the parents, namely mothers, rather than focusing on the social and economic reasons that led to children being disadvantaged (e.g., poverty, inadequate housing, unemployment) (MacIntyre, 1993). This trend continues today as evidenced by the present research.

The Invisibility of the Perpetrator

It is apparent that abused women are almost exclusively the focus of child welfare intervention. Even in situations when the abuse is blatantly perpetrated by the man, he remains absent from the child welfare service plan. Alberta's child welfare legislation mandates intervention when a guardian poses a risk to the child—either by abusing the child or by being unable or unwilling to protect the child from the abuse. Even though a child is deemed in need of protection when physically or emotionally injured by a guardian, this is rarely considered in situations of woman abuse.

> I'm just looking at the types of child abuse [listed in the Act] ... "the guardian is unable or unwilling to protect the child from emotional injury." So I would cite that.

> We would put it [woman abuse] under [the guardian] is unable or unwilling [to protect the child] ... we would defined it as that.

Although the *Child Welfare Act* includes a provision where the guardian is considered to be emotionally injuring a child by exposing them to violence, the workers clearly view the non-abusing guardian as responsible. This may be further exacerbated when the abuser is not the child's legal guardian since the *Child Welfare Act* only addresses maltreatment by the "guardian" of the child. From the following comments, it is clear that little attention is paid to the perpetrators:

> Our main focus is making sure that Mom is okay—Mom has got the parenting skills she needs, Mom has got the therapy so she doesn't get into another abusive relationship. But doing the other stuff [working with the perpetrator] is somewhat difficult, probably difficult until we get funding.

> If they are not the biological dad, they've come into the picture in the last two or three years, I don't work as hard with those guys. I sort of almost push them aside and try to get her to push them aside, because it's harder.

> There is a tendency that if Dad has left the home but still has contact with the kids, to just work with Mom and the kids.... If we work with Mom to make sure she can protect the kids then everything is okay. I have even seen files where, if Dad has left the home, you don't even call Dad. You don't even make any connection with him. So there is a tendency from the Depart-

ment to do that. So I mean, I think it is sort of a narrow focus.

It becomes a lot more difficult and we do have a tendency to leave them [male perpetrators] out because they're trouble.

If they're gone, if the parent has left—I mean it could be an abusive boyfriend, it could be a recent whatever, but they are out of the picture, we're not going to be chasing them to go to some therapy if they're not connected with the family.

From discussions with the eight workers, it appears that the child welfare system may be unable to intervene with perpetrators because it lacks the legislative clout to hold male perpetrators accountable, especially when they are not the biological father or legal guardian of the child. As mentioned previously, the *Child Welfare Act* only mandates intervention with the "guardian" of the child:

Normally we don't do it [work with perpetrator] because once he's out of that home, we can't say, we don't have any clout. With the wife, at least we have her children to use as a leverage point.

We don't have any mandate to just work with the man, alone.

I guess the situation is, who has the children? We have to deal with the family. Who is responsible—the guardian [who] has the child.

Once they've left the family, we don't have any mandate to work with them.

Conclusions and Recommendations

This chapter raises serious questions about how child protection workers intervene in cases where woman abuse occurs. The scant information available suggests that the child welfare legislation that addresses this form of violence may be problematic. This is especially true if the legislation is not accompanied by systems changes, such as increased child welfare funding, expansion of community-based programs for abused women and their children, increased specialized training for child protection workers and more effective responses from the criminal justice system. If child welfare legislation mandates action in cases of woman abuse but effective practice is hindered for various reasons, abused women may find themselves further victimized, rather than protected, by these statutes. Abused women are frequently the focus of child welfare intervention while the actual perpetrators of abuse are ignored or "pushed aside."

Like any policy area, child welfare legislation undergoes ongoing development and change. The following recommendations may assist the child welfare system in better dealing with cases of woman abuse and child protection:

i)   Child welfare jurisdictions should be aware of the direct and indirect effects of including domestic violence in their protective legislation.

Child welfare legislation that includes domestic violence, such as the *Child Welfare Act* of Alberta, can have the opposite effect to the one intended; that is, it may increase the chances of women staying in abusive situations out of fear of losing their children. Abused women are often further victimized by the child welfare system, which considers them to be inadequate parents, because they are perceived as failing to protect their children from the violence. Jurisdictions contemplating amending their child welfare legislation to include domestic violence must be made aware of the possible direct and indirect consequences.

ii)   Child welfare legislation should be assessed from a critical perspective, keeping in mind issues of gender, culture, and class.

The children of women, especially poor women and those from Aboriginal families, are over-represented in the Canadian child welfare system. In cases of domestic violence, women and men are not treated equally. Women are held primarily accountable for the violence and are the focus of case planning. Gender-neutral language falsely assumes that policies, programs and legislation affect everyone in the same way regardless of gender. Child welfare systems should examine policies and practice guidelines for gender bias and should consider men's responsibilities for the well-being of their children. Child welfare policy should clarify that the onus is on the perpetrator to stop the violent behaviour rather than leaving the policy open to interpretation. This may prevent the automatic assumption that the abused woman is responsible for alleviating the situation. This is especially critical because a perpetrator often has ongoing contact with his children, and therefore, he should be held accountable and included in the child welfare case planning. Within child welfare legislation, domestic violence should be named as violence by men against women, reflecting the reality that abusers are almost always male.

iii) Child welfare systems should have the required organizational and legislative resources to effectively respond to situations of woman abuse.

Frequently, policies are ineffective because they represent a mere public display of action—without adequate resources, such policies cannot attain their desired objective (Wharf and McKenzie, 1998). Simply "adding in" domestic violence as an issue of child abuse ignores the organizational constraints that impact on child protection workers' ability to effectively and appropriately respond to woman abuse. As indicated in this study and others, child welfare legislation can be damaging to battered women and their children since this legislation mandates child protection workers to intervene but ignores the fact that they do not have the tools or even the mandate to work with the real perpetrators or to hold them accountable.

We should be implementing policies that effectively address the safety needs of battered women and their children, not ones that punish battered mothers for the risks to their children's safety caused by the batterer. Policies such as Alberta's may make it easy for child protection agencies to inappropriately remove children and lay charges against non-abusing mothers. Developing a legislative and policy context that acknowledges and acts upon issues of woman abuse and offering programs that effectively confront male violence and provide support for women and children are the necessary prerequisites if substantial changes in orientation are to occur. The "psychological father" policy implemented by some American child welfare services to mandate intervention with perpetrators who are neither parents or legal guardians of their victims' children could be incorporated as one way to legitimize a focus on the abuser.

Workers need extensive training in the area of woman abuse so that they understand the dynamics of abuse. Accurate identification of the problems and appropriate service provision can decrease risk and prevent unnecessary out-of-home placements. As mentioned earlier, not all families will require child welfare intervention. A thorough assessment should be conducted to fully understand the strengths, resiliency and other protective factors pertaining to battered women and children. I agree that witnessing violence may have a negative impact on children; however there is a danger in equating witnessing violence with child abuse—all families do not require the level of intervention provided by the child protection system.

Furthermore, one has to question the ability of child welfare agencies to meet the increased demand for service if all children exposed to violence are considered in need of protection. Most child protection agencies complain about the already broad scope of child maltreatment, scarce resources, shortage of foster homes and high staff burn-out. Broadening child welfare's mandate when the system is already overburdened, under-resourced and understaffed will likely worsen these conditions and result in more children being identified without the appropriate resources to help them.

Clearly, some battered women abuse and neglect their children, and child welfare intervention is warranted. However, many abused women are good mothers who are simply caught in bad situations. Sanctioning battered mothers as responsible for the protection of their children is not only unjust but also illogical and ineffective. In situations of woman abuse, good child protection also includes good protection of mothers.

Note

1.   This chapter is based on Kendra Nixon's M.S.W. thesis, supervised by Dr. Jacqueline S. Ismael, Faculty of Social Work, University of Calgary.

Chapter Five

Rewriting Stories
Women's Responses to the Safe Journey Group
Jeannette Moldon[1]

Women who have experienced intimate partner violence require a number of services and support in their journey to end their abuse. These may include counselling, advocacy, education and practical assistance such as finding housing or financial assistance. While I support an integrated intervention model for women who have experienced abuse, this chapter focuses on clinically based interventions, specifically a support group model.

Some writers suggest individual counselling for abused women; however, most recommend a support group format or a combination of group and individual intervention (Campbell, 1986; Dutton, 1992; NiCarthy, Merriam and Coffman, 1984; Sakai, 1991; Stout and McPhail, 1998; Trimpey, 1989; Tutty, Bidgood and Rothery, 1993). Group treatment provides a context that allows women to share their stories and connect with other women with similar experiences and to address personal short- and long-term needs.

Whether offered within or outside shelters, most support group models are based on feminist tenets in which power, patriarchy and privilege are central concepts in analyzing the abuse of women. Important topics to address in group treatment with abused women include the following: legal protection and safety; myths, types, nature and causes of abuse; effects of abuse on self esteem; dealing with anger; communication styles; gender; and focusing on the future (Hartman, 1983; Brown and Dickey, 1992; Jackson and Dilger, 1995; Poels and Berger, 1992; Pressman, 1984). In addition, providing a safe place to share their thoughts and feelings and providing a support system of peers with similar experience is considered crucial. Groups can also rectify the social isolation experienced by many women whose contacts with family and friends may be limited by their partners (Tutty and Rothery, in press).

Most treatment programs for women who have experienced abuse include a substantial focus on knowledge, through a psycho-educational component (Jackson and Dilger, 1995; Abel, 2000). Lenore Walker's (1984) "cycle of violence" is often utilized. This concept identifies a common pattern consisting of three main phases: tension building, followed by the acute abuse incident, and ending with the honeymoon phase. Walker proposes that the pattern recycles throughout abusive relationships. Finally, establishing a personal safety plan is typically an important objective of support group intervention.

Various writers have speculated that effective support groups for abused women increase participants' self-esteem, decrease their depression and enable them to challenge what is believed to be a fixed set of beliefs about women's roles in society (Geller, 1992; Hartman, 1983; NiCarthy et al., 1984). Although groups are arguably one intervention that meets the long-term needs of abused women, little formal research has been conducted to explain how they might be helpful. The paucity of research is especially noticeable when compared to the many evaluations of treatment for the perpetrators of abuse (Tutty, Bidgood and Rothery, 1996). Even Abel's (2000) review of the effectiveness of group treatment found only five studies, all using exploratory research designs (Cox and Stoltenberg, 1991; Holiman and Schilit, 1991; Rinfret-Raynor, Paquet-Deehy, Larouche and Cantin, 1992; Rubin, 1991; Tutty et al., 1993). Most reported significant pre-/post-test improvements in self-esteem, assertiveness, anger levels, locus of control, stress levels and depression. Knowing that group treatment leads to improvements in these areas, however, does not explain how the process works.

The Safe Journey Group

The Safe Journey Group for women was based on a model originally developed by the Family Intervention Project (FIP) at Family Services of Greater Vancouver (1996). The philosophy of the FIP program recognizes a patriarchal system, in which abuse is seen as the result of the unequal expression of power. In practice, the FIP groups apprise women of the oppressive context in which they live, while respecting their own analysis of abuse. Increasing women's safety is paramount. Safety must be defined through each woman's understanding of what safety means, while recognizing that some women may underestimate the risk to their safety. Finally, FIP intervention involves individual and group work, as well as social justice activism in order to dismantle the conditions that favour and perpetuate violence.

The Safe Journey Group (SJG) at Lethbridge Family Services is based on the above tenets and comprises the following themes: reasons for abuse, responsibility for abuse, expectations of relationships, isolation (making the private public and making connections), the impact of abuse (reclaiming self and gaining clarity), and hope and visioning for the future. Specific exercises included in the group program examine both the men's behaviour and the women's experience of the cycle of abuse, understanding power and control and the impact of abuse. The exercises honour women's wisdom in recognizing what they already know, while examining hope and change, and expectations of a relationship. The group is offered over a ten-week period.

How Women Experience the Safe Journey Groups

Eight women who had completed Safe Journey Groups participated in in-depth interviews lasting about one and a half hours. I asked about their experiences in and impressions of the groups. The interviews were conducted at the agency in a private office and all were audiotaped. The tapes were transcribed verbatim and the data analysis utilized standard qualitative methods (Rubin and Rubin, 1995; Coleman and Unrau, 1996).

All eight women were Caucasian with English as their first language; all had been at one time married to male partners who had abused them. The women ranged in age from twenty-six to sixty-one years. At the time of the interviews, six of the eight worked outside their home, another was on a work leave because of a disability (not related to abuse), and one woman was seeking employment. Seven participants had children; six had children currently living with them. Three of the four women whose partners visit their children described the visits as problematic.

Two of the women described emotional abuse from their partner; one reported emotional and financial abuse. The remaining five women had been abused sexually, emotionally and financially. Four of these five were also physically abused. One partner was stalking his ex-wife, phoning her numerous times throughout the day and parking his car outside her home for extended periods.

Only two respondents still lived with their abusive partners while attending the Safe Journey Groups, one of whom continued to experience emotional abuse from her husband. The other was planning to leave her husband in the near future.

The six women no longer in their relationships had all left because of the abuse. Most noted that their partners continue to be emotionally abusive. Each described incidences of emotional abuse, some as recent as the evening before their interview. Leaving inappropriate telephone messages, arguing in front of the children and threatening to withhold money were examples of the continued emotional abuse.

Loss of Self: Views of the Abuse Prior to SJG

Each of the group members reflected on their perceptions of the abuse. Most had interpreted and blamed themselves for their partner's behaviour towards them. Bev and Chris[2] exemplify the experiences that set the stage for joining the SJG:

> I didn't really think that it was abuse. I just thought it was anger and I didn't know what brought on the anger. You don't realize because the put-downs are so gradual. Then in the back of your mind you think that maybe it is me and maybe it is just normal because it happens every day.... I was fearful when he was going into this angry phase. I just thought that it was something that happened in relationships, I was scared.... My self-esteem was so low because of the put-downs, I didn't know who I was. I just thought that I was doing something wrong. (Bev)

> I didn't look at it as abuse because he never hit me, I just looked at it as he was being very cruel with the things he was saying ... and it used to hurt me ... his behaviour. It confused me. I realized within the past five years that he was really abusing me. I went away for treatment, I could no longer work, and all of a sudden I was at home and I did not have that any more. What I was getting was the opposite; I was not efficient, I wasn't smart. I couldn't handle anything. I lost a lot of pride, respect for myself. I lost myself and I needed to get me back. (Chris)

Establishing Safety within the Group

To be effective, groups like SJG must provide a group process and structure that enables the women to establish security and trust. Seven of the eight women had initially felt apprehensive about attending the SJG. Chris described feeling "a little leery about expressing myself in front of strangers," as did Andrea, who stated:

> If you are a private person you don't know if you should share those things. It is one thing to talk to a counsellor about it in a private room. It is another to go share it with a whole group of people you don't know.

Three of the women who were initially nervous had not been physically abused and feared that they would not fit into the group. For example, Bev commented, "I was a bit nervous at first; I thought it would be more for people who were physically abused and not emotionally abused."

In discussing what elements of the group setting enhanced their sense of safety, all of the women identified the surroundings as important. All eight commented that the physical aspects of the room and the location contributed to feeling safe and comfortable. As Andrea discussed:

> It was a safe place to go. Even if one of the ex-partners found us there, it's not like they could just walk in, the door was locked. It was a safe place, which meant that I could put down a few guards. I can sit here with my back to the door. I think it was empowering; he couldn't get to me there.

Debbie noted that the facilitators created a comfortable, safe and caring place to begin to share. The facilitators emphasized that the group members would not have to share anything they were not comfortable with disclosing. Three women described how establishing rules and boundaries at the onset of group provided parameters that reinforced their feelings of safety throughout the group. Kaylee suggested:

> The rules were important, I wasn't judged, not manipulated, not humiliated, just safe ... even my mind. My thoughts are controlled at home; everything that is me is controlled at home. That isn't the way it is here.

Maintaining confidentiality was important to three women.

> I felt very comfortable with the counsellor as far as confidentiality. I was worried about that aspect, because my husband knew I was going to counselling. I just did not want it to be public information. (Chris)

The Group Facilitators
The women described the leaders as providing a weekly structure to the group sessions that contributed to their feeling comfortable. Jana stressed that it was important to her to have an agenda so she would know what was happening and to help the group to focus, learn and move forward in healing. She liked the flexible agenda, which could adapt to any unforeseen occurrences. Kaylee described how the group structure flowed and how this helped her:

> We would have check-in time. That was really good because it gave us a chance to talk about our week and how we were feeling. Also, if we were noticing things in our relationship that

we learned in the group the week before, or if we realized something about ourselves. The leaders created structure around that or else it could take the whole session.

Four women discussed the importance of the facilitators' knowledge of abuse, as well as how they presented the educational components to the group. Chris felt more comfortable knowing that the facilitators were educated about abuse. Kaylee commented that, "it was nice to know they knew what they were talking about; they knew the violence information out there."

Four women commented that the ability of the facilitators to summarize ideas, to question, and/or to listen, contributed to their group experience. These women suggested that the facilitators' communication skills were a key factor in the progress they felt they had made. As Jana stated:

> The facilitators helped me to understand things better. They would have insight, or ask a question in a way that challenged the way I saw it. Whatever you said, no matter how trivial it was, they made it seem important and you were listened to. They had a way of understanding and verbalizing, or summarizing what you said into a coherent way that other people would get what is happening.

Three women commented that having two facilitators was helpful. Kaylee pointed out "if one didn't get it, the other did." Andrea summarized the importance of two facilitators:

> They were both good leaders. They were, I'm sure, very capable of handling a group by themselves. But it really helped to have two. It gave for a really well rounded facilitator. One great big rounded facilitator, rather than two separate entities.

Five women described how the facilitators' disclosure of their own personal experiences was an important component in sharing and connecting in the group. Debbie elaborated:

> They shared their experiences. They had both been in abusive situations too. Theirs were both emotional abuse and mine is mostly emotional abuse and so other people don't see it. So it was really important that they shared.

All eight women felt a bond to the facilitators. As Jana commented:

I was feeling very quickly like they were part of us. It is not like they would go on about their own issues, they would just seem to understand the experience of people on a very deep level and they would bring that knowledge to the rest of the group. So the facilitators were a good experience, different than the group members, but still good.

Three women viewed the facilitators as role models. Bev commented on how their disclosure of past abusive relationships and their subsequent happiness and success in life provided a base for her to re-evaluate her potential. Susan corroborated Bev's feelings:

This person, who is so smart and successful had something like that [abuse] happen to them too. It makes you think that you are not the only one, if they had that happen to them and look where they are now. They were both in good relationships now, with good jobs.

Debbie discussed how the facilitators' balance between strength and gentleness, as well as their ability to "communicate clearly," established them as role models for her.

Sharing in Sisterhood: The Other Group Members
A significant part of the group experience involved connecting with other group members, or, as one of the women described it, "sharing in sisterhood." All eight women commented that sharing their stories of the abuse was important and that it was beneficial to hear the other group members' stories. Bev mentioned that "talking helped to validate what was happening to me. It helped me realize that I shouldn't just ignore it."

Six women discussed how sharing their stories connected them with the others, both through validating each other by listening and by demonstrating understanding, caring and compassion. The women noted similarities between the group members, all being Caucasian and all experiencing abuse. However, some commented on the different forms of abuse that each had experienced. The women who had initially felt uncomfortable with the group composition, later noted that they felt an increased sense of group cohesiveness as time went on. Jana commented:

Although our experiences of abuse were quite different, and I was a lot older than the rest, our healing, fear, anger, loss and different things were all similar. And that was the thread that drew us all together.

Chris remarked that:

> If one person talked about an issue, it would make you realize
> that your situation had common aspects. Sometimes when
> they talked about things, I realized that had happened to me
> too.

The bond of friendship that developed from sharing and connecting was important to everyone's group experience. As Chris stated, "As we began to share our experiences we became friends, because we lived through their lives and our lives." Four women commented that these friendships were the most important aspect of the group experience. Jana referred to the bond as a "sisterhood":

> The one defining aspect of group is that so quickly the feeling
> of camaraderie and sisterhood was there. Whether it was that
> we could all relate to the same problem, whatever was done,
> was setting us up to help us all realize that even though our
> abuse was very, very different, the result of it was still the
> same.

Susan expressed "amazement" that the bond among the group members helped to "change" her and allowed her to feel safe to talk about her experiences.

Three women commented on the importance of humour in the group. Kaylee discussed how one group member in particular could make the others laugh, and she felt that this helped to "break the ice."

> When you say something that might not be funny to someone
> else, but because of the circumstances of group, it's really
> funny to everyone else in the room and you can all laugh
> together. It made you feel closer, like you had this secret with
> other group members.... It is just as important to laugh as to
> cry together. (Andrea)

Women who have experienced abuse are often isolated within their homes, and contact with family, friends and the community is minimal. Four respondents described the group as helpful in reducing isolation. As Kaylee commented:

> I felt so alone. I felt that nobody would understand, so why talk
> about it anyway. It was a very painful time, I felt completely
> isolated. Even though I was away from him, I just continued on
> being abused still, because I was not talking, not getting out,

just like he would have wanted me to. I guess that is why group was so helpful to me—because it got me out, it got me talking about me to other women who understood me. I think that was the most helpful at that time.

Other group members became role models. Listening to the others' experiences of abuse, how they coped and the after-effects modelled strategies that the women could use in their own lives. It also provided a platform to re-assess their own self-worth. As Debbie stated:

I was just amazed at the different strengths each person had ... each one of us. It helped me to see my strengths better because that's what was being destroyed. So first I saw it in them, and then I saw it in myself, that I was strong.

Knowledge Building

Various educational components, including what abuse is, how it happens and issues of power and control, were reported as important aspects of the group experience. A number of the women commented that the educational components enhanced their ability to understand abuse on a personal level.

As mentioned previously, three women had expressed concern because their partner had not physically abused them. One aspect that helped the women resolve their perceptions of difference involved exploring the various forms of abuse and challenging the notion that there is a hierarchy of abuse, with physical abuse as the "worst." Both Andrea and Bev learned that "abuse is abuse." They also noted that the effects of abuse were similar. As Andrea stated, "it all hurts and it all needs to be dealt with." Although Andrea had defined some of her experiences as abusive before joining the group, she learned that she had experienced other forms of abuse: she noted, "I didn't know that a lot of sexual abuse had occurred."

All eight women identified the cycle of abuse as a significant component of their learning experience. Jana commented that, "I was able to watch for the cycle and I could see the pattern. I saw that no matter what I did, he would basically follow the same pattern." Three women discussed the honeymoon phase, realizing that it was, in fact, a part of the cycle. Kaylee noted that, "I never thought that the honeymoon phase was part of the abuse. But I can see how it fits into the whole pattern." Andrea related to the tension-building phase and explosion part of the cycle of abuse. She remembered how she had tried to negotiate her relationship to create peace:

So many years of walking on eggshells.... "Last time this really set him off, so I won't do it again this time." Or, "last time the kids did this and it set him off." In group, you find out that those are his reactions. You don't know what is going to set him off next time, those are his problems, not your problems.

Four women mentioned that developing a safety plan for current or future relationships was a critical group component. Kaylee suggested that even more group time could be spent on this:

It is important to know that I have a way out. If your partner has abused you, having a plan helps you know you can get out. When you are stressed out you don't think of those sorts of things, so it's good that it is done beforehand. I think it would be useful to spend an entire session or at least a little more time on it.

Four women valued learning about the warning signs of abuse, or, as many called them, "red flags" in relationships. Bev suggested that knowing the red flags and not ignoring them or realizing that it was a mistake to believe that you can do something to change the man were important. She speculated that if she had been aware of red flags, she would not have become involved with her partner. Layne commented:

The one [important] aspect was looking at trusting your gut reaction. Often those red flags are a gut reaction, a feeling. Actually, that gut reaction is attached to your knowledge ... so we learned about things that interfere with that gut reaction, like minimizing those red flags.

Five women learned to trust their "gut reaction" and became aware of what interferes with trusting one's intuition. Several described an exercise, referred to as "first voice," that helped them acknowledge their intuition. As Jana noted:

Some of the exercises that we did around listening to your first voice and finding yourself [were important]. Realizing that you lost yourself, your self-esteem, was a gradual thing for me. We did this exercise around taking it back to the first time you didn't listen to your first voice, how you learned how to push it aside, for whatever reasons, and there are many reasons.

Three women discussed other exercises that had helped them to cope with stress and anger in their everyday lives, one being a guided imagery exercise at the beginning of each session that involved imagining a safe place. Chris and Kaylee felt that this helped them deal with stress. As Chris noted, "when I am feeling really stressed about something, like at night when I go to bed, I go to the safe place.... So that was how I had coped with a lot of the situations that came up." Kaylee described a class on anger:

> I learned something really important: that some people store anger and some people let it out, and some people let it out in an unhealthy way. I know that I stored anger so I could be safe; it was my way of coping.... It [the learning component] helped me to release my anger ... and release it constructively ... know with my intuition when I am safe to discuss my anger, and if I can't do it directly, then let it out in other ways, like going for a walk or journaling.

Reclaiming Self

Andrea and Kaylee described Reclaiming Self, the ultimate impact of the group on each woman, as the most important aspect of the SJG. From Andrea's perspective, "The number one thing is that it is okay that this happened. That it is not your fault. I think that the justification in know[ing] that you didn't do anything wrong is just so helpful. It was such a relief."

Learning about the dynamics of abuse helped to alter the criteria by which the women judged themselves and their experiences within their relationship. Five women commented that the educational components of the group enabled each to connect to their own experiences and reduce self-blame. Four women noted that reducing blame helped them to either redefine and renegotiate an existing relationship, or make the decision to leave. Layne and Chris recognized that reducing self-blame allowed them the freedom to function as separate and whole individuals within the relationship by becoming less responsible for their partners' behaviours and moods. Jana and Debbie both noted that understanding that they were not to blame for the abuse and, therefore, cannot change the relationship to stop the abuse, helped them make the decision to leave. As Jana stated:

> I saw that no matter what I did, he would basically follow the same pattern. That helped me to realize that I couldn't do much about this situation, that no matter how much personal development I did, I couldn't change it. That process helped me to leave the relationship, it was a big load off of my shoulders.

The women described a number of ways in which they used what they had learned in the group in their everyday lives. Four respondents referred to the importance of "self-care." Bev commented that this was for her the most important aspect of the SJG. Chris, Susan and Jana discussed the helpfulness of "journaling," "Just to get feelings out, or to write down problems. Sometimes they solve themselves that way."

An important aspect for some involved understanding and connecting to one's emotional self. Four women commented on the process of emerging from emotional numbness, which was facilitated through the validation of their stories in the group. Andrea noted:

> When you experience abuse you close off a lot of emotions because they hurt too much. Then when you are out you have to re-awaken those emotions. Along the way you find out emotions that you didn't know were there sometimes. The group helps you to process some of those feelings. Along the way you find out other things, like, yeah, I have a right to feel angry, I can't do with it what my husband did, but I can still feel it. And you just start to become more alive.

A survivor is defined as an individual who is no longer a victim. The women used various language to describe becoming a survivor, including "recognizing my self-worth, self-esteem, self-trust, independence, inner wisdom, and happiness." A number of the women described how SJG contributed to the process of becoming a survivor and, thereby enabled them to reclaim self. Debbie poignantly described her inability to connect with her sense of self before the SJG and how the group experience has enabled her to view her experiences through an emotional lens. She can now connect to her emotions without ignoring or degrading them:

> Before I went to the group I felt like I was being killed, destroyed. It was a murder of my soul and I was a walking zombie. I wasn't a person.... It [the group] helped me to see my strengths better because that was what was being destroyed. At first I saw it in them and then I saw in myself that I was strong.

Jana described how the group helped restore her self-esteem:

> You don't even know yourself, that inner voice, so your self esteem is zero.... It [the SJG] helped me to see that I had the wisdom and strength to grow and change. That is the first part of the process of self-esteem, and probably the most important.

The Group Framework—"Rewriting Stories"

On reflection, the themes that emerged from the interviews can be viewed as either tools or stages in the process of changing, or "Rewriting Stories." Rewriting stories describes the process of psychological and relational healing that is generated through the group connections. This section re-examines the previously identified themes, placing them within the framework of change and linking them to the work of other feminist authors and researchers in woman abuse.

"Rewriting stories" is a cyclical process of changing positions: a personal journey of rewriting "self" and "relations." It is, as Audre Lorde (1996) would have stated, a process of moving from silence to language to action. The SJG, as such, is a conduit to healing, rather than being the healer itself. For ease of description, the framework is presented here in distinct stages; however, it is important to remember that the stages are not rigid. Women move between the various stages within the framework, each step propelling them to greater self-aware-ness and self-efficacy. Moving through the stages assists women in redefining and reorganizing past interpretations of their experiences from a position of knowing, as well as reclaiming a current voice and self. As Debold, Tolman and Brown state, "the process of constantly revising and re-interpreting our own histories … leads to a shifting 'positionality' with respect to our identity as 'women' or 'knower'" (1996, p. 91). The framework was influenced by self-in-relation theory from the Stone Centre, women's ways of knowing (Belenky, Clinchy, Goldberger and Tarule, 1986), and the writings of Audre Lorde (1996).

The framework has three distinct stages: the lost self, sharing in sisterhood and reclaiming the self (See Figure 5-1). Two tools facilitate the process of moving from stage to stage, establishing safety and knowledge building. The main focus of the themes is connecting to self and others to begin to rewrite stories.

The first stage, entitled the "Lost Self," is characterized by the women's perceptions of their pre-group experiences, which change and adapt over the life of the group. "Establishing Safety" is the tool that enables women to shift to the next stage. The "Sharing in Sister-hood" stage supports the process of connecting to stories of abuse and bonding to other women. Like safety, "Knowledge-Building" is a tool that enables women to define their experiences from a different posi-tion of knowing. The final stage of the framework is "Reclaiming the Self." It is characterized by the women re-appropriating a sense of self that is strong and knowing.

The first stage of the framework, identified as the "lost self" by one of the women, generally describes the women's positions previous to the group. The process of looking back on experiences is one that constantly reshapes and redefines itself. For example, before the group

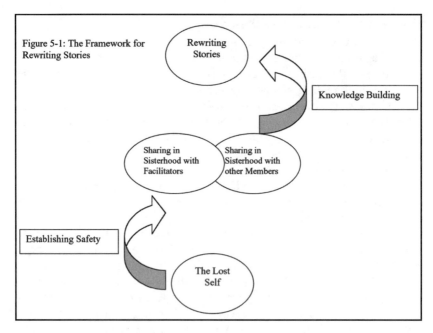

Figure 5-1: The Framework for Rewriting Stories

Rewriting Stories

Knowledge Building

Sharing in Sisterhood with Facilitators

Sharing in Sisterhood with other Members

Establishing Safety

The Lost Self

experience, the women reflected on their stories of abuse from a position of self-blame, whereas later they reflected on these from a position of strength. Prior to group participation, this stage was marked by self-censorship, externally imposed silence, fear, isolation, powerlessness, anxiety and the construction of self by others. Before attending SJG, the women described their sense of knowing as originating outside themselves. It was written for them by authoritative others including the abuser, friends and family and legitimated authorities such as medical and legal professionals, well-meaning counsellors, the self-help literature and educators.

The group participants often used language that spoke of a deficit of knowledge, or "not knowing," when describing their experiences of abuse prior to the group. I would suggest that it was not necessarily "not" knowing, but simply knowing and defining their experiences differently or not being allowed to give voice to their experiences. Silence, in their experience, often meant survival of self and relationships. The process of "not knowing" and "silencing" suggests that abused women are not void of inner knowing nor are they powerless. Instead, such women use survival strategies and cope as best as they can within abusive relationships (Dobash and Dobash, 1988; Gondolf and Fisher, 1988; Yllo, 1993). This stage, then, must not be interpreted as the absence of self, wisdom or knowledge. Rather, the lost-self stage reflects women's pre-group ability to define and redefine their experiences of self in abuse, whether it is through acknowledging strength and/or loss. The redefining is the women's attempts to reconstruct their experiences from the perspective of the realities of self and relations to others, rather than that of an authoritative other.

One tool available to participants is "establishing safety." This tool reflects the necessary conditions to establish comfort, security and trust, or in other words, less fear. It is particularly important because abused women's psychological, mental, relational and physical safety is often compromised. The majority of respondents felt apprehensive about attending SJG. Safety not only represents a precondition to moving forward in the process of rewriting stories but is a consideration throughout the group. Relatively little has been written about safety in groups for abused women. Pressman (1989) suggested that safety should be a "primary consideration." Stout and McPhail (1998) noted that safety is often sadly ignored in the treatment literature for abused women.

The women at SJG discussed the importance of having enough structure to predict the general direction the group and the flexibility to change and adapt to the needs of the group in a "non-threatening" format. As such, safe facilitation requires a balance of structure and collaboration. The facilitators provided knowledge of abuse and expertise in facilitating a group, both of which provided psychological safety for participants.

Another safety consideration is respecting women's decisions about how and when to tell their stories (Wood and Middleman, 1992). The women expanded on the notion of safety to include both confidentiality and location of the group. NiCarthy et al. (1984) proposed that confidentiality is particularly important for abused women because of the risk of danger from an angry (ex)partner.

Safety incorporates physical, emotional and relational aspects of creating a communal environment. This is critical in proceeding to the second stage, "sharing in sisterhood," where women are supported in exchanging, examining and beginning to redefine self through relationships. Woman abuse destroys the supporting bonds between the individual and community. Abuse isolates, separates, divides and often conquers. Further, leaving an abusive relationship exacerbates or continues to destroy community, as it often entails leaving connections to family, friends, religious communities and familiar locations. The group allowed the women to reclaim a sense of "sisterhood" and provided a place of validation and understanding. Establishing a community of women with similar stories helped to liberate the internally censored, isolated and fearful self into a connected, empowered self in progress.

Sharing stories is the conduit of establishing sisterhood. Many of the women felt empowered knowing that they were not the only ones abused by intimate partners. They felt an intense camaraderie with the other group members. The women began to feel validated, initiating a shift away from the isolated and lost self. An abundance of group literature and writing on abused women describes a process similar to sisterhood (Edelwich and Brodsky, 1992; NiCarthy et al., 1984; Pressman, 1989; Stout and McPhail 1998; Tan, Basta, Sullivan and Davidson II, 1995; Whalen, 1996; Yalom, 1975).

A second tool that facilitates movement is "knowledge building." Information provides a foundation for understanding abuse from a different position of "knowing," as well as introducing skills and techniques that women may utilize to become authorities or "knowers" of their own experiences. As a result, the women re-contextualize their experience through a discourse that is broader, empowering and non-blaming.

The goal of knowledge building is to reduce blame and to begin to challenge rationalizations for abuse through the dissemination of information about patriarchy, domination and oppression. Abuse is seen as a symptom of patriarchy rather than as the isolated actions of a few psychologically disturbed males. Through knowledge building, anger and other reactions to understanding oppression are recognized and validated as normal. Learning about different forms of abuse, the cycle of violence and the impact of abuse helped the women to re-contextualize, and therefore, politicize their experiences. Several authors perceive knowledge building as important in groups for abused women (Hartman, 1983; Ibrahim and Herr, 1987; Rubin, 1991; Self-help Canada Series, 1993; Stout and McPhail, 1998; Savage, 1987; Tutty et al., 1993; Wood and Middleman, 1992).

The final stage is defined as "reclaiming the connected self," characterized by the transition from being an "abused" woman to a woman who has experienced abuse. This stage is not isolated from the sharing in sisterhood; the two stages often occur simultaneously and interactively. In this process, women become empowered, finding a "position" of strength and wisdom in self. The connected self, then, changes position from the externally and authoritatively defined to the internally and relationally defined. The respondents described their experience as having found their lost identity and reclaimed their self worth.

As the group evolves, the group members connect to and internalize various aspects of both the process and the content of the group—including safety, sisterhood and knowledge building. They are no longer powerlessly constructed by the abuse but reclaim the facility of rewriting the connected self as strong and knowing women. At this point, women re-interpret and re-appropriate their respective histories.

In summary, the group framework of "Rewriting Stories" is a process of healing that, in turn, rewrites the self. The narrator is the self, the self is relational, or "mutual." The process is constantly in movement, with "positions" shifting and changing throughout time.

Group treatment is important as a setting for abused women to connect with other women with similar experiences. The process (Lost Self, Sharing in Sisterhood and Reclaiming Self) combined with the tools (Safety and Knowledge Building) provides important concepts for designing and implementing group interventions for abused women. Specific aspects such as facilitation (e.g., ability to connect with the participants), safety (e.g., confidentiality, location), group structure and knowledge of abuse are all-important. The women valued the expertise and knowledge of the facilitators with respect to both group content and process. Leaders who have adequate knowledge of woman abuse and the ability to skillfully transmit these ideas form an essential part of the process. Facilitators should have expertise in both group theory and woman abuse. Strong group leaders become role models, modelling equality, connection and collaboration in relationships. Through the appropriate disclosure of their own life experiences they promote hope for the future.

All of the women at SJG were abused. Other than this, they had diverse socio-economic status, education, religion and ages. One would think then, that the group might have difficulty meeting the needs of all of them. Surprisingly, they reported few disappointments. They did, however, make recommendations for future groups.

Two women commented on the size of the group. That particular SJG had started with six but quickly reduced to four members. Both suggested that the experience could have been more interesting with more women. One disappointment reported by five women was that the ten weeks allotted for group was not long enough. When asked what would be a reasonable amount of time, one woman proposed five to six months. Others suggested providing a phase-two group that would focus on self-esteem and "who am I now that I am not abused?"

Power and control is central to women's experiences of abuse. Clinicians should balance groups with enough structure to be predictable, without having so much structure that the group feels controlled and rigid. The SJG experience suggests that a combination of "knowledge building" and "sharing in sisterhood" provides "safety" for the women. Together these components provide the opportunity for women to make significant changes in both their lives and their feelings of self-efficacy.

Notes

1. This chapter is based on Jeannette Moldon's thesis for her Masters of Social Work degree. Her thesis supervisor was Dr. Leslie Tutty.
2. Names have been changed to protect the anonymity of the group members.

Chapter Six

Responding to Lesbian Relationship Violence
An Ethical Challenge[1]
Janice L. Ristock

Recently, in Calgary, Alberta, Deborah Point was found guilty of sec-ond-degree murder and sentenced to twenty years without parole for killing Audrey Trudeau. The jury deliberated for less than an hour to reach their unanimous conclusion. They had heard in graphic detail about a horrific, brutal killing where Deborah Point struck Audrey Trudeau at least fifteen times on the back of her head with an axe, shattering her skull. They learned that Deborah Point had dismem-bered Ms. Trudeau's body and placed the pieces in garbage bags and boxes that she then concealed in a friend's garage. Deborah Point forged cheques and withdrew money from Audrey Trudeau's line of credit to feed her VLT (video lottery terminal) addiction while remain-ing in her house and telling her friends and family members that Audrey had left in a hurry to attend to some business. She also started a new relationship with a woman who moved in with her a few months later. It was five months before the body of Audrey Trudeau was found and Deborah Point was charged.

This case of heartless murder reminds us that women are unfortu-nately capable of extreme violence. It is also a reminder that lethal domestic violence can occur between two women. Yet the court pro-ceedings seemed to ignore the relationship between the two women, while the media coverage of this case often referred to the women as room-mates and did not name this as a case of lesbian domestic vio-lence. Further Audrey Trudeau's family adamantly denied that their daughter was a lesbian, although the Calgary gay and lesbian commu-nity confirmed that Deborah Point was gay and known in the commu-nity. Why was there a lack of attention to the nature of their relationship? Does it matter when abuse in lesbian intimate partnerships such as this is not accurately identified? The varied responses, in my view, reflect the societal homophobia that continues to deny and stigmatize lesbian relationships, making it all the more difficult to understand and respond to violence that occurs within some same-sex relationships.

Although violence in lesbian relationships has been discussed openly within lesbian and feminist communities since the early 1980s, the dangers of publicly acknowledging this issue and contributing to negative stereotypes about lesbians remains a concern. Most of the research conducted to date in this area has focused on documenting the problem of same-sex domestic violence by determining the rates or the prevalence of abuse in order to have it acknowledged by the mainstream. Some researchers (myself included) are interested in creating new understandings in this area by exploring the specificity of lesbian violence; that is, understanding lesbian partner abuse on its own specific terms rather than trying to understand it through comparison to heterosexual partner violence. To do this requires contextualizing such abuse. Account must be taken of how people are located differently in the social world and how racism, classism, heterosexism and sexism affect the causes and consequences of violence and the responses to it.

Mary Eaton (1994), for example, sees the enforced invisibility of lesbians as a factor that must be considered when accounting for abuse. For her, the erasure of lesbians from society's cultural imagination is a unique feature of lesbian oppression, making it different from other forms of social inequality. Furthermore, Claire Renzetti (1998) has been critical of her own early research on lesbian relationship violence as having had a heterosexual bias because she relied on many assumptions arising out of knowledge about heterosexual domestic abuse. Not only have the writings in the area of same-sex abuse been based on hetero-normative assumptions, but they have also centered on white women's experiences, thereby ignoring the effects of systemic power relations like racism, homophobia and heterosexism on abusive relationships (Kanuha, 1990; Waldron, 1996). Similarly, Almeida, Woods, Messineo, Font and Heer (1994) challenge the public and private dichotomy commonly made when addressing forms of violence and suggest that we must look at violence enacted on gays and lesbians and people of colour from different sites and multiple sources. They explain that white heterosexual women may benefit from the public illumination of their private life of intimate violence, but heterosexuals of colour and gays and lesbians do not.

These writings are examples of what is meant by intersectionality. Intersectionality is not an additive model in which one simply adds lesbians to our current understandings of domestic violence; nor is it intended as an approach that falsely compartmentalizes experiences of abuse into separate, special cases (lesbian abuse/women of colour abuse/women with disabilities abuse) while keeping white hetero-sexual women's experiences as the norm and at the forefront. A frame-work of intersectionality includes an analysis of the multiple nature of identity and the interlocking nature of systems of privilege and oppres-sion to show how the categories of race, class, gender and sexuality rely on each other to function within systems of domination (Crenshaw, 1994; Razack, 1998). This framework, then, challenges the either/or binaries within which we often work and demands that researchers develop more contextualized understandings of people's experiences rather than positing all-explanatory grand narratives.

This chapter discusses community-based research[2] utilizing a framework of intersectionality in addition to a theoretical stance that Joan Pennell and I call "feminist links and postmodern interruptions." In this, we research material and discursive and reflexive conditions (that is, we listen to women's stories, we examine the language and concepts used to tell our stories, and we raise questions about our own assumptions and understandings of those stories) as a way of develop-ing a critical and accountable analysis (Ristock and Pennell, 1996; Ristock, in press).

The women involved self-defined as having experienced lesbian[3] relationship violence, including those who defined as victims, perpe-trators, those who felt they fit neither category and those who felt they fit both. Overall, I spoke with a diverse group of women: their ages ranged from eighteen to sixty-six; most identified as lesbian, some as bisexual, two-spirited (a term preferred by many First Nations peoples to describe their gender and/or sexual identity) and heterosexual (a reminder that not all women who have sexual relationships with other women identify with the terms lesbian or bisexual); they included white women and women of colour who identified as First Nations, Metis, South Asian, Asian, Black and Latina. Most were middle- and working-class. Fourteen percent of the women reported disabilities and 18 percent of the interviewees had children. In total, I spoke with 102 women who lived in six Canadian cities: Winnipeg, Vancouver, Calgary, Toronto, London and Halifax.

I also held focus groups in each city. Seventy feminist service providers, including counsellors, shelter workers, therapists and social workers, participated in eight focus groups. Their perspectives were sought because they have been at the forefront of the grass-roots re-sponses to abuse in lesbian relationships. I interviewed ten additional service providers including seven from the United States who worked in organizations or programs dedicated exclusively to lesbian or same-sex partner abuse. The participants with whom I spoke ranged in age from twenty to sixty-three. The majority had a university degree. Most identified as lesbian, a few as heterosexual and bisexual, while some chose not to identify. The participants included white women and women of colour who identified as First Nations, South Asian, Asian and Black (one white man also participated in a focus group). The service providers bring a range of experience in the area of domestic violence of one to thirty years. Most have worked more with heterosexual domestic violence clients than lesbians, and they have seen far fewer gay men. Most worked within organizations (shelters, counselling centers, addiction programs, women's resource centers) while some were therapists in private practice.

The Contexts of Lesbian Relationship Violence

The women whom I interviewed reported many different experiences of abuse including physical (e.g., slapping, hitting, punching, restraining, shoving, using weapons), emotional (e.g., threats to reveal sexual identity, threats to kill, being manipulative), verbal (e.g., constant yelling, put-downs) and sexual. The latter included sexually coercive behaviours, rape/sexual assault and emotional sexual abuse—which involves partners who act in sexually controlling ways that are not consensual, for example, making demeaning comments about their partner's sexual behaviour or body parts. Understandably, the women often found it very difficult to talk about the sexual violence that they had experienced. They commonly expressed shame that another woman could have abused them in this manner. Further, some felt that the term sexual assault did not apply to their experiences even though their partner had sexually violated them, because they associated that language with heterosexuals. For example, Wanda[4] described how her partner would come home and wake her up to assault her:

> She'd come home, wake me up and say "I want to do this or that" and it's like "no," you know. And she used to give me bruises all over my arms when she'd come on the waterbed and hold my arms down … and stuff like that.
> [Would she be forcing you to have sex?] Yeah, now there's something new, I hadn't really saw that.

Wanda had not considered this to be forced sex until describing her experiences in the interview.

Beyond the different forms of abuse, their accounts suggested different patterns of intimate violence that arise from various societal roots and interpersonal dynamics, indicating that not all violence is the same. Rather than creating typologies or correlates of lesbian partner violence, I found it more helpful to consider a range of contextual factors that surround abusive relationships. Efforts to understand violence in lesbian relationships that ignore these contexts run the risk of treating all cases of relationship violence as equivalent and interchangeable when that does not seem to be the case. For example, some social contexts create isolation and invisibility for lesbians and may in turn contribute to the risk of violence.

Invisibility and Isolation: A Context of First Relationships

A strong pattern emerged of women being abused within their first relationships (Ristock, 1998; Ristock, in press). More than half (61) of the women described their first relationship as abusive:

> I lived with two gay men and I always knew that I was a lesbian but there was no community that I was aware of. Gay men, boy, there seemed like there was lots of them, but I didn't know any women and one of these guys knew this lesbian from another city. I didn't get a good impression when I met her the first time, but then she kind of won me over and I guess I was impressionable because I hadn't really met, you know, a real live lesbian. She was about four years older, a former school teacher.… I was really taken by her, you know, this was sort of the first affection that I'd gotten from a woman which I had longed for. (Melissa)

> It was my first relationship. First long-term relationship. But you know I was—I was head over heels madly in love and I thought this is the relationship for life. And it started out really good. This woman was nine years older than myself. It was verbally abusive to start off with and then physically. I was, quite often had black eyes and she tried—she almost killed me once. Strangled me and then this went on for three years.… I was too young and insecure about the whole relationship—gay relationships, whatever. Anybody could have walked all over me. (Ellen)

In many ways this pattern is not surprising given the additional barriers that lesbians (particularly young lesbians) face when initially coming out. Lesbian women enter into a first relationship as outsiders to lesbian communities and are often not plugged in to any support systems. It suggests that violence is part of the cost of a heterosexist context where lesbians may be isolated, unable to access meeting places and often dependent on their first lover for information about living as a lesbian.

Dislocation

Consistent with the context of first relationships being abusive, some participants mentioned similar forms of social vulnerability such as moving to a new city, moving from another country or speaking English as a second language. Rita described the extra pressure that she and her partner felt as recent immigrants who were dislocated, which she believes contributed to the abuse:

> I was around 24, I guess, when I met her and we were both immigrants. She had just been in Canada for about six months. It was a really big thing for her and for me to find a lesbian who was Latina. That was a big thing for us. I could understand what she was going through in terms of learning the language and family.... She considered herself lesbian, but she couldn't really handle the fact that her family was here. She didn't know how to come out to them. The family was starting to pressure her—why was she spending so much time with me? Why was she sleeping over at my place? And I put pressure on her too, it's like we don't see each other as much and I would like to see you more.... The dynamics in our relationship were very weird. I think they were not healthy. At the time we were also best friends, we didn't have no supports whatsoever and we didn't know any other lesbian either.

She is not excusing her abusive partner's behaviour but describing the isolating context in which they found themselves.

Homophobia and the Closet

Gays, lesbians and transgendered people have all experienced the impact of living in a homophobic culture. Even though considerable gains have been made in human rights and in visibility, many lesbians remain closeted, feeling that they must hide their sexuality from some people even when they are "out" to others. We also know that within abusive relationships, abusers threaten to "out" their partner as a way of exerting power in the relationship (Renzetti, 1992; Scherzer, 1998). For many of the women I interviewed, the power of homophobic threats was often connected to the context of the closet (created by institutional homophobia) within which many lesbians still live. Forty-eight women stated that the closet was a factor within their abusive relationship. This was most evident for women who lived in small, rural or northern locations where there may be more dangers in being out. This context added to their isolation and invisibility leaving them unable to speak with anyone about what they were going through. For example, a college teacher in a rural town reported that her partner used her history of losing a job because she was gay as a way to keep her in the relationship:

> I'm living in this small town, population five, six thousand. I was very concerned about people knowing that I'm gay because I just don't want the harassment. I meet this woman with two children ... and within two weeks I realize that there is something seriously wrong with this woman. She's got a mean streak. And I was like, I'm outta there, this isn't good. She goes "if you even think about leaving or breaking up this relationship, I will ruin your life." Meanwhile I have the memory of this other harassment when I was an elementary school teacher and I don't want to have to leave this small town because it takes a particularly long time, in education, to get your career on track again. (Kelly)

Kelly remained in this relationship, that became progressively more abusive, for eighteen months. In another example, a woman and her abusive partner lived in a small, rural town and worked together in the same workplace where they were not out and were thought of as room-mates:

> I would go to work, of course, with bizarre excuses for why I had a black eye or this, that or the other thing. And we weren't out—we worked together—we weren't out at work. So we were always just like buddies and "Ha, ha this happened." You know? Whatever ... and she was a Baptist minister's daughter. (Mary Ann)

Violence was normalized in another context, which included the use of drugs and alcohol, a history of previous partner abuse and the experience of a lifetime of general abuse in a context of poverty and racism. Each of these contextual factors may increase one's risk of experiencing violence. This does not, however, suggest that they caused the violence.

A Lifetime of Violence: Racism and Poverty
A recurrent feature of the women's accounts was the context of a lifetime of violence that occurred on many levels. One woman spoke specifically about the context of colonization. Ruth identified as Metis and her partner as Aboriginal. Each had experienced sexual violence and racial violence, as had their families:

> My mother is Cree and her parents were really devastated by
> residential schools and my mother grew up in an extremely
> violent, abusive, alcoholic home. And I remember thinking
> that I was living out that legacy. I recall thinking … it was like
> two opposites. At one hand it was like this is the legacy that we
> carry. It is to be expected, I mean what do you expect from an
> Indian? Right? Just because we are so inundated with violence,
> we become normalized to it. And on the other hand, I also
> knew this is not normal, this is not acceptable.

Ruth also spoke of understanding her abusive partner's feeling of
powerlessness that she believes contributed to her abusiveness. This
came from a context of racism in a way that did not affect her because
she could often pass as white. The impact of racism and colonization
demonstrates the ways in which personal stories are linked to historical contexts that influence and shape people's lives. Their experiences
are not shaped solely through racism but reveal the way experiences of
racism, sexism and homophobia intersect and affect each other in
contexts such as sexual abuse, child abuse and/or domestic violence.

Thus, there are a number of differing contexts in which women
spoke about violence in their relationships. Although not exhaustive
and at times overlapping, these contexts were prominent in creating
isolation and invisibility for lesbians or in normalizing abusiveness.
Each shows the specific ways in which violence takes hold and is
reinforced within a larger context of social structures that create and
sustain inequalities and disadvantages. In focusing on social contexts I
am moving away from "either/or" categories or typologies that we have
often relied on to understand violence but which only end up excluding
some women's experiences or making them marginal. The women
spoke to me of a range and diversity of violence: they also revealed a
similar diversity in the dynamics of abuse within the relationships.

Relationship Dynamics: Shifting Power and Fighting Back

Many of the women described relationship dynamics that resemble
Walker's (1984) "cycle-of-violence" model, often described in abusive
heterosexual relationships. In this cycle, violence occurs in a predictable fashion and intensifies over time. Part of the cycle includes a
period of calm following an acute battering episode. In this relationship dynamic there is clearly a perpetrator and a victim. Perpetrators
are seen as using abusive tactics as a way to gain and maintain power
and control over their partner throughout the relationship. Several
women also mentioned the status of their partner that contributed to
their power over them. For example, women's abusive partners included their therapists, professors and bosses. In one case, the abuser

was a police officer, meaning that the respondent could not call the police for support. In another case, the abuser worked at a battered women's shelter thus limiting the abused's options for support.

However, other women spoke not of a cycle but a constant pattern of abuse—often daily emotional abuse that had existed throughout their relationship. Some mentioned that the physical violence increased whenever they tried to leave the relationship or to resist the abuser's control. Two women described an increase in the violence when they were pregnant. These are more familiar stories of what has come to be understood as abusive relationship dynamics.

Yet other women spoke of less predictable and even fluctuating power dynamics within their relationships. In their accounts, power does not reside fully in one person (the abuser) but was instead relational, as is evident in the following examples:

> The imbalance of power between a man and a woman is constant just because a man has privilege in society. And so there's always going to be that, whether he's going to chose to work on it or not. Different factors may change some aspects of power but that power will remain constant. Whereas with two women, I think that the power fluctuates more ... there's more variables involved that can change. I know with my relationship with S. at certain times she was so weak I had the power. I remember at certain times I would say things and I would go, "Oh my god, I can't believe I said that." And I think I was verbally abusive to her in several ways. (Rhonda)

> I don't like getting beat up and so you defend yourself physically. And your adrenaline runs. You get an energy, no matter what size you are, you have more power and strength. I would say to her, you know, "Take your arm off me or whatever, the hair pulling or whatever was going on, or I will break your arm." And I knew I would; I was ready to break her arm. But what that does to you basically is it makes you taste—and it is a literal taste in the mouth—the adrenaline of your own violence. And it doesn't go away the next day. It's a really amazing, bitterish, aftertaste thing. It's a horror and I resent the fact that another human being would bring me to a place where I would do that. (Michaela)

The perspectives of Michaela and Rhonda suggest that we must explore the meanings of the concepts "power" and "control" that are most often used to describe relationship violence. Further, the focus on shifting power dynamics within abusive relationships has implications for how we understand the categories of victim and perpetrator. For example, the image of a victim as pure, innocent and helpless looms large in dominant culture and makes it difficult to speak about agency, strength, resiliency and even a "taste" for revenge as other features of being a victim (Lamb, 1999).

Yet many of the women with whom I spoke were not passive victims: thirty-eight described physically fighting back within their abusive relationships. There may be more opportunities for both partners to use violence in lesbian relationships because of their relatively similar physical sizes and strengths and because of the construction of femininity (unlike masculinity) as something which is not to be feared. Perhaps it is this particular, gendered dynamic of two women that leads to different relations of power. For example, seven women described fighting back with the intent to hurt their partner and to retaliate, while twenty-three spoke of fighting back in self-defence throughout the relationship and, of those, six indicated that their efforts at self-defence became a desire to hurt their partner. Nine women spoke of fighting back once or twice, often towards the end of the relationship (usually a single episode when they reached a point where they had had enough) while a few others tried fighting back to stop the violence but stopped because it did not work. Some women commented that they were abused in one relationship and then became controlling in the next. Thus, there was great diversity and complexity in what constituted fighting back and in women's reasons for fighting back, including fighting back as a coping strategy, a form of resistance, an intentional act to cause harm and/or a self-defence reaction.

One young twenty-five-year-old woman, Kirstie, whose mother had just died when she became involved in a relationship, provided the following account: " I was very attracted to her and I was also trying to fill a void with my mom not being there. I just put all of my energy into this person." She described her partner as a very jealous person, who was always phoning to check up on her at work. The relationship began as emotionally and verbally abusive and then became physically abusive:

> We would be okay as long as we didn't drink. We both started drinking heavily. She was dealing with stuff from her past and I was dealing with my grief and now my grief was shut off because I was just so involved with my relationship and just trying to appease her. I stopped grieving totally and the unfortunate thing is I stopped it in an angry period and I guess my anger took over. We started out getting destructive. We just started cursing each other out throwing things around, destroying things. The turning point for me was when I couldn't

take it any more. I started becoming, I guess aggressive with her when she had taken a picture of my mom and she tried to burn it. I couldn't believe that she did that.

Their relationship worsened with further episodes of physical violence and with each partner upping the ante of intensity. Kirstie's partner then left her and became involved with another woman. Kirstie began stalking her, punctured her car tires and also threatened to kill her or commit suicide. She explained the shift in her behaviour as occurring because her partner attacked her core of vulnerability at that moment—a picture of her dead mother.

Another woman described fighting back that became retaliation because she knew what was going to happen next and thought that she needed to defend herself in order to not be further victimized. Barb had experienced so much violence in her life, she said she had "victim written all over my forehead." This is how she explained the fighting back:

> And the third time, I knew it was going to happen again, I beat her up. And I couldn't stop—I'm not that kind of person at all. I've never done anything like that before or since. I did it on the street and I think that's why I did it, because I knew there were people around in case. And I was angry.

In her story, Barb both hurts her partner and protects her by staging the violence where someone might intervene and stop her.

Each woman's story reflects different reasons for the shifting power dynamics and yet all suggest a resistance to being controlled. Too often complex dynamics between women, such as when there is fighting back, have been labelled as mutual abuse. Like "innocent victim," "mutual abuse" is clearly a problematic term, in this case one that assumes equal power, motivation and intention to harm when that is not what is being described. Do motivation and intention matter in all instances of partner violence? How do we decide? How do we assess acts of resistance or differing intentions within each partner when there is fighting back or when abuse continues? Grappling with these complexities in abusive-relationship dynamics is necessary not only for understanding lesbian partner violence but also for developing effective responses.

Social Services for Lesbians

Rather than homogenizing lesbian partner violence I have attempted to show the range and diversity of the violence that the women describe. Yet this diversity is not necessarily reflected in the responses that social service agencies have developed. More often, the assumption is that there is only one type of relationship violence: lesbian abuse is simply the same as heterosexual abuse. Too often the women that I interviewed felt they had few options. They were more likely to turn to friends (64) and counsellors (57) for support and less likely to call the police (14) or go to a shelter (6) because they assumed that the police were likely to be homophobic and/or racist and that battered women's shelters are only for heterosexuals. These women showed strength and courage as they were often forced to cope on their own while struggling within a hetero-normative culture that marginalizes and misreads intimate relationships between women.

The Responses of Feminist Service Providers

There has been a varied response to lesbian domestic violence across Canada. Feminist and women's services with some gay/lesbian/bisexual/transgendered services in major urban centres have primarily attempted to respond to this issue. Agencies have typically responded by offering support groups for survivors, producing educational brochures and/or forming coalitions that actively attempt to raise awareness and coordinate effective responses between shelters, police and grass-roots organizations. In larger Canadian and American urban centres with visible gay and lesbian communities, some services have been developed solely for lesbian, queer or same-sex domestic violence. In smaller locations one individual lesbian or feminist may offer resources and supports. Both organizations and individual service providers face many difficulties, such as a lack of funding for any "queer" issue, as well as great concerns over confidentiality, homophobia and a backlash against feminism. Many agencies are further restricted by their funding sources and mandates, leaving them unable to develop the necessary responses.

This issue also raises political tensions. For example, if women's antiviolence services are responding to lesbian relationship violence because they can more easily add lesbians into their existing programs, who will respond to the needs of gay men or transgendered people in abusive relationships? Where can they go for a safe shelter, for example? Are agencies that serve heterosexual women, in fact, welcoming of lesbians? Further, for feminists, a gender-based explanation of domestic violence is clearly inappropriate for explaining lesbian partner violence. Given the challenges of gender-based domestic violence theory, the question arises as to how feminist service providers currently understand and respond to abuse in lesbian relationships.

Based on my discussions with feminist service providers, the majority provides services for victims either within agencies or in private-practice counselling with very few working specifically with women who are abusive. In fact many women's services have a mandate to work only with victims, leaving women who are abusive with few, if any, options for assistance. However, service providers are making adjustments to established models originally designed for heterosexual domestic violence. Innovations in service provision include couple assessment (determining who is abusing whom in the absence of a clear gender power differential), running support groups for lesbians who have been abused and creating more specific programs for lesbian survivors of abuse rather than merely having a lesbian woman join a heterosexual woman's program. Most are aware of how this issue complicates feminist understandings of male violence against women because they have to confront the fact that women can be both victims and abusers.

The Constellation of Power and Control Discourse

The focus group discussions with service providers confirmed many of the patterns identified in the interviews with lesbian respondents. An interesting finding was that women who came for counselling seldom identified abuse as the presenting problem, but raised other issues, such as self-esteem, depression or relationship problems as their primary concern. One implication of this finding is that service providers not working in battered women's services or shelters are often in the position of being the one to define the relationship as abusive. Their perceptions become influential in how a woman will understand her own experience and in determining the kind of support she will receive. I was particularly interested in the language and concepts—the discourses—that feminist providers used in talking about lesbian relationship violence since our language informs, shapes and limits what we know and think about violence. For example, we can only understand someone's experiences of relationship violence through representation—that is, how a woman tells her story or how a counsellor reports it. We understand that representation within our own web of meanings, which include our beliefs about violence, lesbians and women's bodies. We need to reflect on these constructions and discourses in order to become more conscious of the categories we use to express our assumptions—categories that might include the experiences of some women while excluding others and which may naturalize certain forms of violence while repressing knowledge of others. Many of the service providers and lesbians that I interviewed commented that we do not have a language to express certain aspects of lesbian culture (because it is not dominant) and, therefore, cannot fully understand or articulate certain features of lesbian relationships and violence.

In the focus group discussions there was a reliance on a dominant discourse when speaking about abusive relationships—what I call "the constellation of power and control." I call this a discourse because it entails a consciously and unconsciously accepted structure of language, concepts and assumptions that are used in domestic violence work, positioning people and framing our understandings. The "power and control constellation" is the foundational discourse for making assessments of abusive relationships and for understanding all forms of abuse. It is partially conceptualized in a diagram called the power and control wheel—with power and control at the hub, and the spokes of the wheel representing different forms of abuse, all held together by physical and sexual violence (or their threat) (Pence and Paymar, 1993). We are utilizing this constellation when we identify power and control (rightly or wrongly) as the core feature of an abusive relationship and assume that we will find in that relationship a pattern of fear and intimidation that restricts the abused woman's movements and thoughts and traumatizes her. It is not that power and control are not features of abusive relationships, but we do rely on a simplified version with a corresponding set of assumptions in order to distinguish a victim and a perpetrator rather than exploring contextualized relations of power. All of the service providers with whom I spoke used the terms "power and control" to describe dynamics that they look for when assessing the presence of abuse. For example:

> Domestic violence is a power and control dynamic—I don't really care about what somebody's sexual orientation is, or what their gender identification is, um, I'm just looking at power and control dynamics. (a service provider in a feminist agency with a lesbian program)

As this person suggests, when identifying relationship violence the focus then centres on the decontextualized couple and what one partner does to another. When this model becomes widely applied to all cases of domestic violence a homogenizing process occurs so that it no longer matters what "somebody's sexual orientation is, or what their gender identification is." In other words, rather than looking at the relationship in a context and unravelling the layers of complexity and specificity, the focus shifts to the traumatizing effects of violence.

The power and control constellation includes a focus on listening for evidence of fear to help determine who the victim is and then treating the trauma experienced by that woman. The following comment provides an example:

> I think the word fear comes to mind. Does the other partner really feel fearful that the person is going to retaliate or be physically abusive or so on? (Focus group)

A focus on the common effects of relationship violence allows for a continued focus on the similarities of heterosexual and lesbian relationship violence. This was also discussed in the focus group:

> Domestic violence assumes marriage, assumes spousal relationships, assumes a lot of things that do not apply to lesbians ... so there is a problem with using that paradigm of domestic violence: the whole issue of heterosexism and homophobia in the relationship and sort of projecting maleness onto a partner or projecting issues around an abusive mother onto a partner with same-sex abuse. So I think those are issues—how those issues play out in the relationships—the issues of race and class—the power dynamics in the relationships—I think they are different than they are when I'm working with heterosexuals. But a fist is a fist. So the other part is entirely the same. Violence is violence and trauma is trauma. [murmurs of agreement from the group] (Focus group)

The statement that "violence is violence and trauma is trauma" resurrects a "trauma talk" discourse, as Jeanne Marecek (1999) describes it, to its dominant place, disavowing the significance of different contexts and making it difficult to explore the problems and inadequacies of current models that explain domestic violence.

The "constellation of power and control" discourse offers a compelling framework, which assumes that power is an entity held by one person (not necessarily related to their status) and used against another to control them (the assumed motivation). Further, fear is the acknowledged context of the relational dynamic and trauma is the expected consequence or effect (often seen as being compounded by a lifelong experience of patriarchal violence against women). Feminist service providers then focus their efforts on responding to the traumatized victim/survivor. This power-and-control discourse includes the rigid binary concept of victim/perpetrator. Feminist service providers are accustomed to working within clear dichotomies of women as victims and men as oppressors/perpetrators. In this context, the man holds power, which is supported by a patriarchal context and used against the woman/victim. Yet the context of lesbian relationships and woman-to-woman abuse remains invisible and conveniently erased by this overarching assumption of sameness, as are the varied contexts, reactions and responses to violence. For example, this binary model of power and control/victim and perpetrator cannot account for the abuse by an unemployed waitress of a woman who is a prosperous chartered accountant. Nor can it account for the dynamics of a power shift which occurs when a victim retaliates with physical violence. Finally, it cannot capture those incidents in which a woman might be both a victim and a perpetrator; for example, a victim of a hate crime and a perpetrator of physical violence in her relationship. Furthermore, what if a woman does not express fear as part of her experience of being abused? Yet the incentive to preserve this clearly oversimplifying discourse is strong, since it constitutes the rationale for the institutions we have developed, with great effort, to respond to heterosexual domestic violence.

Despite the emphasis on maintaining this unifying discourse, the focus group participants identified some differences between lesbian and heterosexual abuse. For example, they noted that homophobia may be used as a threat within abusive lesbian relationships, and they remarked on the way that a larger context of heterosexism can isolate a couple and make it difficult for them to access support. However, they were clearly not comfortable in speculating further in differences which might challenge dominant feminist thinking about domestic violence. For example, one focus group discussion was exploring a situation in which a victim both sought revenge and tried to hurt her partner. The participants quickly reframed this as self-protection and allowed no room for the possibility that a victim could have additional motivators of retaliation and anger.

> We would call that self-protection because we would talk about how they'd been oppressed—that that oppression is always invisible and they're saying, "I don't deserve this, I'm a human being," and that would be where the retaliation comes from—we would put that in self-protection. (Focus group)

In focusing only on the effects of violence and in staying with universalist feminist assumptions of what motivates the perpetrator, we can erase and ignore any dissonance between heterosexual domestic violence theory and lesbians' experience of domestic violence: in this way we can continue with our current practices.

Power

At other times the service providers did acknowledge some complexities and differing contexts of relationship violence. For example, questions about layers of power relations were sometimes raised:

> I think racism is another thing we don't talk about—the ways white women might use power over their partner who is a woman of colour—there is power and control there.... How do we talk about that and then also talk about other power complexities in the relationship? (Focus group)

Here, someone is struggling with the dominant view of power as a fixed entity resting in one person. This view of power and the rigid victim/perpetrator binary cannot account for the example where a white woman may be both a victim of physical abuse and a perpetrator of racist violence in a relationship.

Overall, the discussions revealed the normative discourses that feminist service providers both employ and, at times, struggle against. They show the investment we have in maintaining certain dominant feminist understandings about relationship violence ("abuse is abuse") while also trying to acknowledge differences and respond effectively. In conducting this research as a lesbian and a feminist, I too struggled with how best to understand and respond to same-sex relationship violence, while also keeping a strong focus on the overwhelming patterns of male violence against women in our society. After listening to so many women's stories, I believe that we need to move away from rigid, binary notions of victim and perpetrator, power and control, and those homogenizing understandings that stress the similarities of domestic violence. We must instead shift our focus to how power operates in women's lives within specific contexts. This requires an examination of structural, personal and relational levels of power. Women who are acting abusively must be held accountable but we must also move from making simple moral judgments (pronouncing someone as abusive/ bad or victimized/good) to taking strong ethical stances (seeing how power operates with all of its complexities and responding to it). It is important to note that feminists have understood the why's of power by naming oppressive structural conditions such as racism, colonization, patriarchy and heterosexism. We now need to place more attention on the how's of power relations that are produced by these conditions and that require multiple and varied responses. That can include, for example, women who have been victims of male sexual assault and perpetrators of relationship violence or women who have been abused in one relationship and act abusively in the next.

Conclusion

My interviews with lesbians who have experienced abuse and my discussions with feminist service providers both show (in different ways) that we need analyses in the field of relationship violence that account for the complexities of women's lives rather than enforcing universality and a simplifying of experiences. Overall, our greatest challenge is to take an ethical stance that sees and responds to violence in relationships which have a multiplicity of identities and exist within differing contexts and spaces, on their own terms and with all of their particularities. For example, lesbian relationships involve two women (with all the constructions of femininity and lesbianism at play) within a larger context that still renders sexual relationships between women invisible and throughout which circulate the differing social and personal effects of heterosexism, racism, sexism and classism on relationships and on women's subjectivities. We need to understand those spaces, how power circulates through, between and around them, and not just focus on how the effects of abuse are all the same. As one woman whom I interviewed said:

> I feel like I can't talk about it, I mean how many therapists/ social service providers are going to understand queer, s/m, abuse, intersexed, interracial [all features of her abusive relationship]—It's too complicated, there is too much explaining that I'd have to do. (Natalie)

My hope is that, despite the difficulties, we can embrace this ethical challenge of understanding and responding to complexities, nuances and differences. At the same time, we need to remember that violence in lesbian relationships is a political issue that can be used against lesbians to support homophobic views that see our relationships as deviant and unhealthy. It is important, therefore, that we become actively involved in supporting anti-oppressive efforts and that we continue to see relationship violence as a political issue facing our communities.

Notes

1. This chapter is based on my book, *No More Secrets: Violence in Lesbian Relationships*. New York: Routledge Press (in press).
2. I am grateful to the women who so generously gave of their time and spirit to participate in this research. This research was supported by a grant from the Lesbian Health Fund of the Gay and Lesbian Medical Association and from the Social Sciences and Humanities Research Council of Canada. Many thanks to Vycki Anastasiadis, Caroline Fusco, Cindy Holmes, Natasha Hurley, Lois Greiger, Beth Jackson, Kavita Joshi, Kristi Kemp, Jan Mitchell and Betsy Szilock who worked as research assistants on the project. Also thanks to the Rainbow Resource Centre in Winnipeg; The FREDA Centre for Research on Violence Against Women and Children, Battered Women's Support Services and The Centre for GLBT's and Allies in Vancouver; The David Kelley GLBT Counseling Program and Women's Health in Women's Hands in Toronto; the Sexual Assault Centre in London, Ontario; Peer Support Services for Battered Women in Calgary; and the Avalon Sexual Assault Centre in Halifax, Nova Scotia, for providing me with space and contacts and advertising this research; special thanks to Myrna Carlsen, Laurie Chesley, Karlene Faith, Donna Huen, Yasmin Jiwani, Louise MacPherson, Marg McGill, Kathleen O'Connell, Jane Oxenbury, Donna Wilson, Rae-Ann Woods. The author is grateful to CatherineTaylor for her editorial comments and on-going support. Ad-

dress correspondence to: Janice L. Ristock, Women's Studies Program, University of Manitoba, Winnipeg, Manitoba, Canada, R3T 2N2. E-mail: ristock@cc.umanitoba.ca

3.   I use the term lesbian relationships to include women who are involved in an intimate relationship with another woman. However, not all women in relationships with other women identify as lesbians and might prefer terms such as bisexual, butch, femme, gay, two-spirited, dyke or queer. Further, other women may more strongly identify with their ethnic or cultural background rather than with their sexual identity.

4.   The names and initials used in this report are all pseudonyms.

Chapter Seven

Challenges and Future Directions

Leslie Tutty and Carolyn Goard

This book not only presents current research about abused women in Canada but also allows us to reflect on the nature of abuse and how we currently respond to the needs of women affected by intimate partner violence and to their children. In spite of almost three decades of awareness about this critical issue, there remains considerable controversy about what to label as abusive and how to assist both the victims and perpetrators.

Despite the now widespread acknowledgment that intimate partner violence is a significant problem in Canadian society, it is still often difficult for women both to acknowledge that their intimate partner is abusing them and to seek assistance. We have not yet developed a clear delineation of when couples are in conflict and when their behaviour is abusive. Unfortunately, conflicted and divorcing couples now commonly use the term "abuse" to describe any of their partner's behaviour that they do not like, in much the same way that individuals use the term "depressed" to describe days when they are feeling blue. Moreover, some media advertisements intended to educate about domestic abuse unintentionally result in the general public downplaying its significance. This is so because television is hampered by significant ethical concerns in its depiction of abusive behaviour. It cannot accurately show significant physical assaults or denigrating verbal abuse, so the portrayals often resemble marital conflict between equals. This has resulted in skepticism from some quarters about the significance of woman abuse and misunderstanding about its chronic and degrading nature.

Another barrier to acknowledging woman abuse remains internal to the individual—facing the realization that one's husband, lover or boyfriend is behaving abusively. Intimate partners rarely behave abusively all the time, as Walker's (1984) "cycle of violence" so usefully describes. Even when abuse is physical, women are often persuaded to forgive by promises that it will not happen again.

But what do we make of long-standing abuse that is emotional or psychological in nature rather than physical? One of the reasons that we now seldom use the term "battered" is that it excludes non-physical violence, such as derogatory or degrading comments, threats of violence or death threats to other family members or pets. Numerous abused women have commented that they find the emotional abuse harder to bear than the physical. The significant effects of ongoing emotional abuse are dramatically portrayed in this book by the support group member in Jeanette Moldon's study who described it as the "murder of my soul." Yet many women who have "only" experienced emotional abuse do not perceive it as abuse, nor do they see that they might benefit from assistance.

Acknowledging the negative impact of emotional abuse has opened up two issues that have created dilemmas in keeping the profile of abused women front and centre. The first is the idea that exposure of children to the abuse of their mother by their father constitutes abuse in and of itself. Such exposure is a form of emotional abuse, and, as Kendra Nixon's chapter so clearly identifies, this revelation has created significant debate and tension between advocates for abused women and child protection workers. Should child witnesses who have not themselves been physically abused be considered in need of protection by child welfare authorities? This question was raised over a decade and a half ago in Ontario. Although arguments both for and against this provision were cited, one of the disadvantages noted was that mandatory reporting of each child victim could "damage [a] fragile life-line for women and children as well as hamper an open sharing of information between shelter staff and child protection workers" (Jaffe, Wilson, Cameron, Zajc and Wolfe, 1987, pp. 4–5), since a possible consequence would be that women might refuse to seek refuge in transition houses, fearing that their children would be taken from them.

The central issue should be not whether, but how, to intervene with women whose children have been exposed to marital violence. The importance of intervention is unquestionable when children are physically abused. But it is also critical when children are exposed to traumatic events including threats to kill them or their mother, or when they behave in extreme or harmful ways, such as threatening suicide as the two young boys in Chapter Two did. Rather than becoming combative, child protection workers and women's advocates must listen to and dialogue with each other.

A second issue is what, for lack of a better term, we call "husband abuse." The few studies available on this phenomenon report less frequent and less severe physical violence. The majority of the incidents constitute emotional abuse (Tutty, 1999a). Among the significant differences from woman abuse are the following factors: men are less likely to feel fearful, their lives are not typically threatened, and any physical abuse is infrequent and episodic rather than ongoing. Abused men are also considerably less visible to those working in the front lines who typically assist large numbers of abused women: medical, police and shelter personnel. Canadian crime statistics from 1996, for example, noted that 89 percent of victims of spouse assaults were women and about 11 percent were male (Pottie-Bunge and Levett, 1998).

While not intending to downplay any form of abuse, nor to suggest that men abused by intimate partners do not also need support, a major concern is that resources to assist abused men will be taken from funding now available to help abused women. Canadian scholars such as Walter DeKeseredy and Linda MacLeod (1997) worry that "proving" that women's aggression is equal to men's could lead to abandoning society's support for abused women. This could occur through withdrawal of funding for shelters, diverting moneys to "battered men" and increasing arrests of women where mandatory-arrest policies exist. Recently, in a western Canadian city, a group for men abused by women partners was financed by decreasing the number of groups offered to women victims.

The voices of men's advocates claiming that the "family violence" debate should be gender-neutral because husband abuse is as serious and widespread as woman abuse have become stronger in the past several years. Provincial transition house associations, government representatives and shelter directors are often questioned about the lack of services for men. Some agencies have been asked to shift the language in violence-awareness materials to be gender-neutral. In 2000, a men's advocate group won a challenge under Alberta human rights legislation against a family service agency in Edmonton, whose brochures for group intervention focused on male violence against women and did not mention that women partners may also abuse men. The agency, a non-profit organization, decided not to fight the ruling that their brochures were discriminatory because the challenge had already been so costly in both time and financial resources.

It is tempting at times to argue for a hierarchy of abuse, with emotional as the least important and physical as more worthy of attention, as had been anticipated by some of the support group members in Jeanette Moldon's study. However, emotional abuse can, indeed, have devastating consequences and create terror in its wake. Consider the following circumstances described by Brianne, one of the women whose story we presented in the introduction to the book:

> He may not have lived with me, but he had free rein to come and go as he pleased. You can't lock him out because his

> specialty was B and E's when he was younger. So even when I tried to lock him out one time, he climbed into the house. Because I have so many kids, I always was afraid of guns. He would never blatantly bring the gun to my house. But he would always let me know that there was a gun in the house and I never knew where. So if he got mad and looked like he was going somewhere, like the basement, it scared me.

Brianne understandably felt both frightened and controlled by the implicit threat presented by Greg hiding a gun in her home.

The chapter on shelters reminds us of another factor, the degrading and ongoing serious nature of the physical abuse that some men perpetrate on their partners. A number of the shelter residents disclosed physical and emotional abuse with life-threatening consequences that most of us could not imagine enduring. Some women, although safe in shelter when interviewed, also recognized that their partners would never let them live independently, and although they were safe momentarily, once they left the shelter system, their lives would be at risk once again.

Janice Ristock's chapter on abuse in lesbian relationships adds considerable depth to an issue that has really only surfaced in the past decade. Identifying that some women in lesbian relationships also behave abusively compels us to re-examine some of our core beliefs about abuse in intimate partner relationships. Previous characterizations of the abuser as male and the victim as female allowed us to ignore the fact that women may also utilize power in abusive ways. Lesbian battering challenges views about abuse that have been based solely on heterosexual relationships in which men are the typical perpetrators (Ristock, 1997). In lesbian partnerships it is not necessarily easy to identify who perpetrates abuse: the abuser may be small and petite but violent, and the partner who is assaulted may be larger and look stereotypically more powerful.

Ristock's discussion about the need to differentiate when violent behaviour may be in self-defence and when purposeful or revengeful is one that can be applied to heterosexual couples, although the distinction remains difficult to make. After thirty years of addressing the issue, the "one size fits all" view of violence in intimate relationships needs to be dismantled and replaced with a more accurate and varied view of the complex circumstances of couple relationships. We need to remain open to differences in abuse within intimate partner relationships. Only then will we develop services that truly provide protection and assist people to change.

The System's Response to Woman Abuse

Other chapters in the book focus more directly on services and agency responses to intimate partner violence. Tutty and Rothery provided the resident's perspectives on how shelters are helpful; Jane Ursel examined in depth the different facets of the justice response to abused women at Winnipeg's Family Violence Court. Kendra Nixon presented an analysis of child protection workers' beliefs and practices when confronted with information that children were exposed to their father's abuse of their mother. Finally, Jeanette Moldon interviewed women about their impressions of one of the interventions first developed for woman abuse—support groups. Each chapter outlined current practice, and presented common dilemmas faced by each system, which raise questions about when and how to intervene.

In the remainder of this chapter we revisit each of these systems using the stories of Brianne and Sheryl to illustrate the complexities of the lives of two abused women and how seeking assistance did not always result in the anticipated reaction. Their narratives identify some of the challenges that women face, especially since many deal with more than one of these systems.

Shelters

Shelters for abused women sprang from the grass roots of the women's movement to become organizations that are supported by provincial governments across Canada. After almost thirty years of service in some communities, shelters are seen as integral in offering safety and crisis intervention to women and children affected by violence (Tutty, in press). As noted by the respondents in Chapter Two, women see the safety offered by shelters as their primary purpose. Their importance has been validated by communities through financial help and donations and by many citizens who, for example, express outrage on hearing about the number of women turned away from shelters.

Brianne valued her stay in an Ontario emergency shelter and used the Canadian shelter network to travel to Alberta to reside in another transition homes far away from Greg. With the assistance of the shelter staff and outreach program she found an apartment and began to establish a new life for herself and her children. However, as Brianne describes:

> I lasted two months and I went back. I started to feel guilty about separating him from the kids. I figured he had to know the worth of being in a family. But how could he? He doesn't know himself.... I was still afraid of him. Even on the bus on the way back to him I started to get afraid.

Once again, although Greg did not live with Brianne or their children, another violent incident occurred and Brianne decided to leave for good. She travelled back to Alberta and the shelter outreach staff assisted her to find a new apartment in a second-stage shelter.

In contrast, Sheryl had a negative reaction to the shelter staff, who contacted the child welfare authorities, who subsequently took her children into care. With respect to shelters, Sheryl said:

> I would tell someone to think long and hard before going to a shelter, quite honestly. Exhaust every other resource, do anything you can to stay out of the shelter. As great a place as it is, the future ramifications may not be something that you anticipate. I wish someone had told me. I can honestly say that I really do not believe that there's anything that could justify having Child Welfare take my children away.

While transition houses are generally regarded as necessary for the safety of women and children, several pressures significantly challenge how effectively they can offer services. One is the belief that shelters are a sufficient solution to woman abuse; that all one needs to do is to offer emergency support. Many members of the public do not understand that the transition to a life free of abuse is unlikely to occur in a three-week visit to an emergency woman's shelter. Women and children need additional services that address their long-term needs for either coping within an assaultive relationship or leaving one. Also, the expectations of what shelters can offer have increased over the years. They are expected to provide follow-up, outreach, prevention programs, support groups and public education, but generally without financial support for these "extras." While such programs are generally considered helpful, if we truly acknowledge the complexities of leaving an abusive partner, we must also ask whether there are enough services available for abused women and their children, beyond shelter.

In addition to providing safety and linking women to community resources while they are in shelter residence, what more can shelters do to assist women? Over half of the women in Chapter Two reported traumatic reactions to the event that led to shelter entry, such that they had high levels of avoidance and intrusive memories. These reactions interfere with one's ability to be emotionally and cognitively available to problem-solve and make changes in one's life. On reflection, and partly in reaction to the results of the research, one of the shelters, the Sheriff King Home, began offering several modalities of counselling specific to Post Traumatic Stress Disorder symptoms. They also trained the shelter staff in utilizing a trauma perspective and are currently collecting data with respect to the success of these interventions. In the words of a former shelter resident:

> I have a connection between my intellectual brain and emotional brain that didn't exist before EMDR [Eye-Movement Desensitization and Reprocessing]. I no longer suffer from severe anxiety, and can now ride the bus and go places on my own. It is such a feeling of freedom! I feel that although it will take time, eventually the two will get closer and I will be more balanced that way. I know what it is like to feel emotional pain and much as I hate it I know that going through emotions helps you get rid of the trauma.

Support Groups for Women
Groups for abused women, such as the Safe Journey Groups described in Chapter Five, are a mainstay of the system response whether offered in shelters or in community-based agencies. Such groups have been given relatively little research attention, especially when compared to the resources focused on researching groups for male perpetrators (Tutty and Rothery, in press). While groups for men are undeniably critical, the experiences of the women in the Safe Journey Groups reflect the corrosion of self-esteem that is too commonly the result of living with an abusive partner. These effects do not magically disappear upon leaving an abusive relationship but often interfere in women's lives for years afterwards. The early evidence on support and therapy groups reminds us that dealing with intimate partner violence is not simply about assisting women to leave abusive relationships. Woman abuse affects the entire family long after that system supposedly changes or dissolves. Support groups can have a substantial impact on the process of reclaiming the self that was damaged in the abusive partnership.

Sheryl spoke positively about the support groups that she had attended, "They have lots of support groups ... that's great! I've gone to a few myself, and I've even facilitated a few."

Brianne had attended a group in Alberta before she reconciled with Greg. She commented:

> I always went to group on Tuesdays, and then [snaps fingers] I took off. In the last couple of groups before I left, I started mentioning that I had spoken to him. So when I got back [after reconciling and then breaking up with Greg], it's a bit of a pride-swallowing thing to say, "Okay, guys, it's me again. I know I screwed up, but can I ask for help again? Can you guys be there again?" And it was no problem. So the biggest surprise

is that I don't feel at all like I was being judged.... I thought everything through so much that it would be kind of hard to surprise me. Except I was surprised that I would get the help again.

The Justice Response to Woman Abuse

Legislative responses to partner abuse have focused primarily on attempts to increase the safety of women and their children. Until the recent introduction of a federal Canadian law creating a new offence of criminal harassment to address stalking behaviour, women could not access protection from the police or the courts, since nothing physical had yet occurred (Rodgers, 1994). Another example is provincial civil legislation such as the Saskatchewan *Victims of Domestic Violence Assistance Act* that allows abused women to stay in their homes while the men are removed (Davis et al., 1994) through the provision of twenty-four-hour emergency intervention orders available from select justices of the peace. These orders can offer a victim exclusive possession of the home, allow police to remove an abuser from the premises, restrict communication or direct police to accompany either the victim or abuser to supervise the removal of personal belongings. Similar legislation has been adopted in Prince Edward Island, Alberta and Manitoba. A major concern about such legislation is whether women can be kept safe in their homes. However, removing the partner is only deemed appropriate where the risk is considered low: if a woman or children were in danger they would be moved to a shelter.

Nevertheless, the justice system response to domestic violence has been of long-standing concern to women victims and those who provide them with services. As noted in Chapter Three, it is common for partners to attempt to coerce women to drop charges or not cooperate with police. Many domestic cases do not proceed to court and, when they do, defence lawyers and others may treat women witnesses poorly. Even when found guilty, men's sentences are typically relatively light and do not reflect the ongoing nature of the assaults.

Sheryl had a negative experience with the police after her husband sexually assaulted her. As she described:

> I went to the hospital to get evidence in case I wanted to charge him. I needed to see if I was OK and if I did decide to charge him, I would need to get evidence. They wouldn't do a rape kit, not because they weren't sympathetic. They were very nice about it, but they wouldn't do a rape kit because it wasn't necessary to prove the identity. The doctor said, "it doesn't matter. He can say it was consensual; it wouldn't prove anything." Then, I phoned the RCMP.... I lived in a small town. I

was still undecided as to whether I wanted to charge Corey. I told them the story and made it quite clear that I was undecided about whether to lay charges. He said to me at one point that he believed that a rape had taken place. He had no problem pressing charges if I decided to and he would get back to me in a couple of hours to see what I decided to do. He came back with a female police officer. They put a little bit more pressure on me; he wasn't quite as nice. Then, two hours later after that, they phoned me and said that they didn't believe me a bit, and if I pursued this, they'd press mischief charges against me.

Brianne had contact with both the police, though not at her initiative, and the courts. Her experience with the police was during the final incident before she left Greg for good. Greg was becoming increasingly upset. Her friend asked if she should phone the police:

I said, no, because I had never called the police. She said, "If it gets too crazy I have no choice. I have to call the police." But the people upstairs called. When the police came I was upstairs, 'cause I had run out of the house again with the kids. The police pulled him out and took him overnight and let him out again. [Interviewer: Did they confiscate the gun?] No, They didn't search. They asked me if he was armed and I said, "There's a great possibility that he could be," so they just grabbed him and took him out and that was it. Kept him overnight. Let him go the next day. I was scared to death. I was sure that he would be held at least until trial. After all the years he had been in [jail] and always for violent crimes.... And finally I do the right thing, I press charges and once you press charges then it's like you've betrayed them ultimately. If you press charges, it means you're on the side of the law.

Brianne feared for her life after this and once again sought the safety of the shelter. However, she still had to face the prospect of testifying in court in a city that, at that time had no specialized domestic violence court:

I didn't end up testifying in the end. I was being prepared [in a court preparation program] because he had pled not guilty, of course. It's rare that a man will plead guilty. And if he pleads not guilty it's really hard to prove because there's hardly ever any witnesses other than people who have heard something, and then how can you prove it? It's really tough to pin them for that. But at the last second, when we were all called in, he changed his plea to guilty because I had filled out a victim impact statement. I just let it all out [laughs] about all the other times on top of this one and I guess he figured, "Oh-oh. If she's here and she's going to do it, I don't want to go back to jail yet, at least not in that way." He pled guilty to assault and death threats! He pled guilty to it and he got no time! He got two years probation with follow-up with a probation officer and he got one hundred hours of community work to be done within a year. What a joke.

Brianne was devastated by the court's failure to significantly punish Greg for the violence he had inflicted on her and the children. She believed that she had no choice but to leave the province for her own safety. Both she and Sheryl felt that, not only had the justice system failed them, but also the system had ultimately supported their partners by not taking the violence seriously.

Research assessing the efficacy of a variety of law enforcement, justice and community responses to domestic violence is crucial in deterring further violence and ensuring the ongoing safety of victims and their children. The continued collection of justice data, such as described in Chapter Three on the Winnipeg Family violence court, provides invaluable information about whether and what aspects of the justice response work and what might be adopted by other jurisdictions.[1]

Child Welfare's Response

As mentioned previously, Kendra Nixon's chapter about child protection workers' response to children exposed to woman abuse raises further dilemmas. As Nixon effectively presents, such legislation was originally adopted to protect children, identifying exposure to parental violence as abusive in and of itself. Yet the impact of the legislation has been to pit shelter workers, most often the advocates for women, against child protection workers, the advocates for children, in unproductive ways.

Sheryl's children were apprehended by child welfare authorities, who had been alerted by the shelter staff. She describes the subsequent court hearing about whether the children should be made temporary wards:

> People stood up in court and said that the children were not physically, sexually or emotionally abused. It hasn't made a difference so far. Child Welfare was going for a temporary guardianship order for six months. The judge granted it after

hearing the testimony. Child Welfare says that you can take children away for domestic disharmony and/or domestic violence. If that's a reason that people can take your children away from you, then why would you go to a shelter so that you can give them more ammunition? I could understand if I had beaten my children or if I'd done something, but I stayed home with my kids, and all I did was go to a shelter.

Sheryl's comments echo the concerns raised in Chapter Four about the possible consequences if women learn that their children could be apprehended if they seek emergency shelter. Shelter workers are often concerned about the effect of abuse on children. Since over three-quarters of women come to transition houses with children, often with several, children make up the majority of residents (Statistics Canada, 1999/2000). Mothers must deal not only with their own emotional distress and trauma but with their children's reactions and trauma as well. Children's difficult behaviours that surface in shelters however are not simply related to abuse but to the transition and loss of much of what is familiar—school, friends, activities and family members. Copping (1996) confirmed that, over the course of their stay in one of five Ontario shelters, children's difficult behaviour gradually improved, suggesting that much of it was in reaction to the many changes they had endured.

In a 1996 Canadian study of women's perceptions of their children's needs in a shelter (Bennett, Dawe and Power), a number of respondents commented on the importance of help from the staff both in addressing their child's issues and in providing information on parenting. Teaching parenting skills is considered controversial by some who perceive it as disempowering mothers by implicitly criticizing their behaviour. However, offering parenting programs allows the staff to support mothers, rather than criticizing or offering advice in front of the children.

Over the past decade, numerous programs, either in shelters or community-based programs, have been developed to assist children exposed to woman abuse. The Transition Home Survey (Statistics Canada, 1999/2000) found that over half of Canadian shelters (54 percent) offer such group counselling programs. Many provide parallel programs for parents to assist them in interpreting their child's behaviour as a reaction to witnessing abuse and to develop more effective methods of dealing with these responses (Tutty and Wagar, 1994). Such group programs are considered essential and are offered in a way that does not blame parents nor hold them responsible for factors over which they have little control, such as their partner's abusive behaviour. Promoting such interventions when a child has not been physically abused but is reacting to having lived in an abusive household is one way of supporting rather than threatening abused women.

Further research and debate about child welfare interventions in cases of children being exposed to marital violence will be important so that mothers are not revictimized by another aspect of the system, while their partners' behaviours are ignored. As well, children will not be traumatized by being separated from the mothers, who have often been the mainstay in their protection.

Challenges for the Future

As this book relates, although the issue of woman abuse has finally gained and maintained the attention of the Canadian public, we face a number of challenges in the next twenty years. Resources are typically the first challenge and, while shelters are available in most large urban centres, we have no clear answers to the question of how to best ensure the safety of abused women in small, rural and remote areas. Nor is it likely that shelters, as now conceptualized, will be the model adapted for smaller centres. The development of specialized justice responses that speed the entry of domestic assault cases to court and allow opportunities for men to be mandated to treatment appear promising. Yet, there continue to be women and children who are not adequately protected by shelters, mandated treatment for men and specialized legal interventions.

How were Brianne and Sheryl doing at last contact? Brianne had been living in a second-stage shelter for the past five months. She was taking a job-training course and her children were settled in school in their new community. Brianne no longer felt any pull to return to a relationship with Greg for either her sake or her children's.

Sheryl was heartbroken about her children having been taken into temporary care by Child Welfare. She resolved to do everything she could to get them back, working at a full-time job, enrolling in support groups and taking parenting courses. She and Corey did not reconcile, although there were times when Sheryl was tempted to do so because she was lonely. However, the child welfare workers had made it clear that if the couple reunited, the children would not be returned. The last time we spoke with Sheryl the hearing to determine the children's fate had not yet been held.

We must remain open to hearing the voices of abused women such as Brianne and Sheryl to ensure that the system's responses address the needs of all of the individuals affected by the abuse. It is critical to engage and recognize the strengths that it takes both to cope in an abusive partnership and to leave one. To the extent that professionals, whether counsellors, police, shelter staff or child protection workers, see themselves as intervening to save "victims," we ultimately negate their coping skills and discourage them. We also deny the bonds to the perpetrator—emotional, financial and familial—that resulted in their adapting and attempting to change the family from within. We also fail to acknowledge gaps in services and difficulties finding support. Unless we understand and accommodate their complex realities, we cannot assist women in more than superficial ways—ways that in the long run will lead them to rejecting our support.

The extent to which North American society has acknowledged and provided services from justice, social services and therapeutic perspectives to abused women and their children over the past thirty years is impressive. It has undoubtedly saved lives. Unfortunately though, women and their children continue to die at the hands of intimate partners. We must resist the pressure to view the problem of woman abuse as having been exaggerated and services over-funded. If it has no other impact, we hope that the voices of the women in this book will encourage all to remember the serious nature of woman abuse. Furthermore, may it remind all of us to do whatever we can to empower women to ensure their own safety and their children's.

Note

1. RESOLVE recently received funding from the Social Sciences and Humanities Research Council to compare the justice response to domestic violence in five jurisdictions across the three prairie provinces. The research will include the Winnipeg full court, Calgary's domestic violence docket court (Homefront) and three other centres without specialized courts, but with other services such as domestic abuse follow-up teams (Edmonton). This will permit a comparison across a variety of programs to assess what model and components work most effectively. The safety of women and their perceptions of the justice system are a key component of the research.

References

Abel, E. (2000). Psychosocial treatment for battered women: A review of empirical research. *Research on Social Work Practice,* 10(1), 55–77.

Alexander, M.J., and Muenzenmaier, K. (1998). Trauma, addiction, and recovery. In B. Levin, A. Blanch, and A. Jennings (Eds.), *Women's mental health services: A public health perspective* (pp. 215–39). Thousand Oaks, CA: Sage.

Almeida, R., Woods, R., Messineo, T., Font, R., and Heer, C. (1994). Violence in the lives of the racially different: A public and private dilemma. *Journal of Feminist Family Therapy,* 5 (3/4), 99–126.

Armitage, A. (1993). The policy and legislative context. In B. Wharf (Ed.), *Rethinking child welfare in Canada* (pp. 37–63). Toronto, ON: Oxford University Press.

Aron, L., and Olson, K. (1997). Efforts by child welfare agencies to address domestic violence. *Public Welfare,* 55, 4–13.

Astin, M., Lawrence, K., and Foy, D. (1993). Posttraumatic stress disorder among battered women: Risk and resiliency factors. *Violence and Victims,* 8(1), 17–28.

Astin, M.C., Ogland-Hand, S.M., Coleman, E.M., and Foy, D. (1995). Posttraumatic stress disorder and childhood abuse in battered women: Comparisons with maritally distressed women. *Journal of Consulting and Clinical Psychology,* 63(2), 308–312.

Beeman, S., and Edleson, J. (2000). Collaborating on family safety: Challenges for children's and women's advocates. In R. Geffner, P. Jaffe, and M. Sudermann (Eds.), *Children exposed to domestic violence: Current issues in research, intervention, prevention, and policy development* (pp. 345–58). New York: Haworth.

Beeman, S., Hagemeister, A. and Edleson, J. (1999). Child protection and battered women's services: From conflict to collaboration. *Child Maltreatment,* 4, 116–26.

Belenky, M.F, Clinchy, B.M., Goldberger, N.R, and Tarule, J.M. (1986). *Women's ways of knowing: The development of self, voice and mind.* New York: Basic Books.

Bennett, L., Dawe, D., and Power, J. (1996). *Women's perceptions of their children's needs in women's shelters.* Research report. St John's, NF: Memorial University.

Bowker, L., and Maurer, L. (1985). The importance of sheltering in the lives of battered women. *Response to the Victimization of Women and Children*, 8(1), 2–8.

Breci, M., and Simons, R. (1998). An examination of organizational and individual factors that influence police response to domestic disturbance. *Journal of Police Science and Administration* 15(2), 93–104.

Breton, M., and Bunston, T. (1992). Physical and sexual violence in the lives of homeless women. *Canadian Journal of Community Mental Health*, 11(1), 29–43.

Brown, P., and Dickey, C. (1992). Critical reflections in groups with abused women. *Affilia*, 7(3), 57–71.

Buel, S.M. (1988). Mandatory arrest for domestic violence. *Harvard Women's Law Journal*, 11, 213–26.

Callahan, M. (1993). Feminist approaches: Women recreate child welfare. In B. Wharf (Ed.), *Rethinking child welfare in Canada* (pp. 172–209). Toronto: Oxford University Press.

Campbell, J.C. (1986). A survivor group for battered women. *Advances in Nursing Science*, 8, 13–20.

Campbell, J.C., and Soeken, K.L. (1999). Forced sex and intimate partner violence: Effects on women's risk and women's health. *Violence Against Women*, 5(9), 1017–35.

Canada Mortgage and Housing Corporation (1994). *Draft final report on the evaluation of the Project Haven Program and update on the Next Step Program activities*. Ottawa, ON: CMHC.

Cannon, J., and Sparks, J. (1989). Shelters—An alternative to violence: A psychosocial case study. *Journal of Community Psychology*, 17, 203–13.

Carlson, B. (1977). Battered women and their assailants. *Social Work*, 22, 455–60.

_____. (1984). Causes and maintenance of domestic violence: An ecological analysis. *Social Service Review*, 569–87.

Carroll, J. (1994). The protection of children exposed to marital violence. *Child Abuse Review*, 3, 6–14.

Carter, J., and Schechter, S. (1997). *Child abuse and domestic violence: Creating community partnerships for safe families*. Family Violence Prevention Fund. http://www.fvpf.org/fund/materials/speakup/child_abuse.

Cascardi, M., and O'Leary, D. (1992). Depressive symptomatology, self-esteem and self-blame in battered women. *Journal of Family Violence*, 7(4), 249–59.

Charles, N. (1994). The housing needs of women and children escaping domestic violence. *Journal of Social Policy*, 23(4), 465–87.

Coleman, F.L. (1997). Stalking behavior and the cycle of domestic violence. *Journal of Interpersonal Violence*, 12(3), 420–32.

Coleman, H., and Unrau, Y. (1996). Phase three: Analyzing your data. In L.M. Tutty, M.A. Rothery, and R.M. Grinnell Jr. (Eds.), *Qualitative research for social workers* (pp. 88–119). Toronto: Allyn and Bacon.

Copping, V.E. (1996). Beyond over- and under-control: Behavioral observations of shelter children. *Journal of Family Violence*, 11(1), 41–57.

Corsilles, A. (1994). No-drop cases in the prosecution of domestic violence cases: Guarantee to action or dangerous solution? *Fordham Law Review*, 63 (3), 853–81.

Costin, L. (1985). Introduction. *Child Welfare,* 64, 197-201.

Cox, J.W., and Stoltenberg, C.D. (1991). Evaluation of a treatment program for battered wives. *Journal of Family Violence,* 6(4), 395–413.

Crenshaw, K.W. (1994). Mapping the margins: Intersectionality, identity politics, and violence against women of color. In M.A. Fineman and R. Mykitiuk (Eds.), *The public nature of private violence* (pp. 93–118). New York: Routledge.

Davis, L., Hagen, J.L., and Early, T.J. (1994). Social services for battered women: Are they adequate, accessible and appropriate? *Social Work,* 39 (6), 695–704.

Davis, R., Smith, B., and Nickles, L. (1998). The deterrent effect of prosecuting domestic violence misdemeanors. *Crime and Delinquency,* 44(3), 434–42.

Dawson, R. (1990). *Child sexual abuse: Investigation and assessment.* Toronto: Institute for the Prevention of Child Abuse.

Debold, E., Tolman, D. and Brown, L.K. (1996). Embodying knowledge, knowing desire: Authority and split subjectivities in girls' epistemological development. In N. Goldberger, J. Tarule, B. Clinchy, and M. Belenky (Eds.), *Knowledge, difference and power: Essays inspired by women's ways of knowing* (pp. 85–125). New York: Basic Books.

DeKeseredy, W., and Hinch, R. (1991). *Woman abuse: Sociological perspectives.* Toronto: Thompson Educational Publishing.

DeKeseredy, W., and MacLeod, L. (1997). *Woman abuse: A sociological story.* Toronto: Harcourt and Brace.

Dobash, R.E., and Dobash, R. (1979). *Violence against wives.* New York: Free Press.

_____. (1988). Research as social action: The struggle for battered women. In K. Yllo and M. Bograd (Eds.), *Feminist perspectives on wife abuse* (pp. 51–74). Beverly Hills, CA: Sage.

Dobash, R.E, Dobash, R.P., Cavanagh, K. and Lewis, R. (2000). *Changing violent men.* Newbury Park, CA: Sage.

Dolon, R., Hendricks, J., and Meagher, S. (1986). Police practices and attitudes toward domestic violence. *Journal of Police Science and Administration* 14(3),187–92.

Dutton, D., and Painter, S. (1993). The battered woman syndrome: Effects of severity and intermittency of abuse. *American Journal of Orthopsychiatry,* 63(4), 614–22.

Dutton, M. (1992). *Empowering and healing the battered woman.* New York: Springer.

Dziegielewski, S.F., Resnick, C., and Krause, N.B. (1996). Shelter-based crisis intervention with battered women. In A.R. Roberts (Ed.), *Helping battered women: New perspectives and remedies* (pp.159–87). New York: Oxford University Press.

Eaton, M. (1994). Abuse by any other name: Feminism, difference and intralesbian violence. In M.A. Fineman and R. Mykitiuk (Eds.), *The public nature of private violence* (pp. 93–118). New York: Routledge.

Echlin, C., and Marshall, L. (1994). Child protection services for children of battered women. In P. Jaffe, E. Peled, and J. Edleson (Eds.), *Ending the cycle of violence —Community responses to children of battered women* (pp. 170–85) Thousand Oaks, CA: Sage.

Echlin, C., and Osthoff, B. (2000). Child protection workers and battered women's advocates working together to end violence against women and children. In R. Geffner, P. Jaffe, and M. Sudermann (Eds.), *Children exposed to domestic violence: Current issues in research, intervention, prevention, and policy development* (pp. 207–19). New York: Haworth.

Edleson, J. (1998). Responsible mothers and invisible men: Child protection in the case of adult domestic violence. *Journal of Interpersonal Violence, 13,* 294–98.

_____. (1999). The overlap between child maltreatment and woman battering. *Violence Against Women, 5,* 134–55.

Edleson, J., and Beeman, S. (2000). *Responding to the co-occurrence of child maltreatment and adult domestic violence in Hennepin County.* http://www.mincava.umn.edu/link/finrport.asp

Edelwich, J., and Brodsky, A. (1992). *Group counseling for the resistant client: A practical guide to group process.* New York: Lexington.

Ellis, D. (1992). Woman abuse among separated and divorced women: The relevance of social support. In E.C. Viano (Ed.), *Intimate violence: Interdisciplinary perspectives* (pp. 177–89). Washington, DC: Hemisphere.

Ericson, R.V., and Baranek, P.M. (1982). *The ordering of justice: A study of accused persons as dependents in the criminal process.* Toronto: University of Toronto Press.

"Failure to Protect" Working Group (2000). Charging battered mothers with "failure to protect": Still blaming the victim. *Fordham Urban Law Journal, 27,* 849–73.

Family Violence Intervention Project. (1996). *A manual of ideas and practice with women who experience abuse.* Vancouver, BC: Family Violence Prevention Division, Health Canada.

Fantuzzo, J., and Lindquist, C. (1989). The effects of observing conjugal violence on children: A review and analysis of research methodology. *Journal of Family Violence, 4*(1), 77–94.

Farmer, E., and Owen, M. (1995). *Child protection practice: private risks and public remedies.* London, U.K.: HMSO.

Ferraro, K.J., and Pope, L. (1993). Irreconcilable differences: Battered women, police, and the law. In N.Z. Hilton (Ed.), *Legal responses to wife assault: Current trends and evaluation* (pp. 96–123). Newbury Park, CA: Sage.

Fields, M. (1978). Wife beating: Government intervention, policies, and practices. In U.S. Commission on Civil Rights, *Battered women: Issues of public policy.* Washington, DC: U.S. Commission on Civil Rights.

Findlater, J., and Kelly, S. (1999). Reframing child safety in Michigan: Building collaboration among domestic violence, family preservation, and child protection services. *Child Maltreatment, 4,* 167–74.

Fitzgerald, R. (1999). *Family violence: A statistical profile 1999.* Ottawa, Canada: Statistics Canada.

Fleury, R., Sullivan, C., and Bybee, D. (2000). When ending the relationship does not end the violence. *Violence Against Women, 6,* 1363–83.

Ford, D.A. (1991). Prosecution as a victim power source: A note on empowering women in their violent conjugal relationships. *Law and Society Review, 25* (2), 313–34.

Ford, D.A., and Burke, M.J. (1987). Victim initiated criminal complaints for wife battery: An assessment of motives. Paper presented at the Third

National Conference for Family Violence Researchers, Durham, New Hampshire.

Ford, D.A., and Regoli, M.J. (1993). *The Indianapolis Domestic Violence Prosecution Experiment*. Final Report, NIJ Grant no. 86-IJ-CX-0012. Indianapolis: Indiana University, and Washington, DC: US Department of Justice, National Institute of Justice, and US Department of Health and Human Services, National Institute of Mental Health.

Friday, P., Metzgar, S, and Walters, D. (1991). Policing domestic violence: Perceptions, experience, and reality. *Criminal Justice Review*, 16(2), 198–213.

Geller, J.A. (1992). *Breaking destructive patterns: Multiple strategies for treating partner abuse*. New York: Free Press.

Gelles, R. (1976). Abused wives: Why do they stay? *Journal of Marriage and the Family*, 38(4), 659–68.

Gelles, R., and Straus, M. (1979). Determinants of violence in the family: Toward a theoretical integration. In W. Burr, R. Hill, F.I. Nye, and I.L. Reiss (Eds.), *Contemporary theories about the family* (Vol. 1, pp. 549–81). New York: Free Press.

Genova L.R. (1981). Plea bargaining: In the end, who really benefits? *Canadian Criminology Forum*, 4, 30–44.

Giles-Sims, J. (1983). *Wife-battering: A systems theory approach*. New York: Guilford Press.

Gleason, W. (1993). Mental disorders in battered women: An empirical study. *Violence and Victims*, 8(1), 53–68.

Goldstein, H. (1977). *Policing a free society*. Cambridge, MA: Ballinger.

Gondolf, E. (1998). *Assessing woman battering in mental health services*. Thousand Oaks, CA: Sage.

Gondolf, E., and Fisher, E. (1988). *Battered women as survivors: An alternative to treating learned helplessness*. Lexington, MA: Lexington.

Goolkasian, G. (1986). *Confronting domestic violence: A guide for criminal justice agencies*. Issues and Practices, NCJ 101680. Washington, DC: US Department of Justice, National Institute of Justice.

Gordon, J.S. (1996). Community services for abused women: A review of perceived usefulness and efficacy. *Journal of Family Violence*, 11(4), 315–29.

Gordon, L. (1988). *Heroes of their own lives: The politics and history of family violence*. New York: Penguin Books.

Greaves, L., Heapy, N., and Wylie, A. (1988). Advocacy services: Reassessing the profile and needs of battered women. *Canadian Journal of Community Mental Health*, 7(2), 39–51.

Haddix, A. (1996). Unseen victims: Acknowledging the effects of domestic violence on children through statutory termination of parental rights. *California Law Review*, 84, 757–815.

Harrell, A., and Smith, B. (1998). Effects of restraining orders on domestic violence victims. *Legal interventions in family violence: Research findings and policy implications*. U.S. Dept. of Justice. (NCJ 171666)

Hartik, L. (1982). *Identification of personality characteristics and self-concept factors of battered wives*. Palo Alto, CA: R & E Research.

Hartman, S. (1983). A self-help group for women in abusive relationships. *Social Work With Groups*, 6, 133–34.

Hebert, C., and Foley, J. (1997). Building shelter, taking down walls. In G. Burford and J. Symonds (Eds.), *Ties that bind: An anthology of social work and social welfare in Newfoundland and Labrador* (pp. 187–221). St John's, NF: Jesperson.

Hershorn, M., and Rosenbaum, A. (1985). Children of marital violence: A closer look at the unintended victims. *American Journal of Orthopsychiatry,* 55, 260–66.

Hilberman, E., and Munson, K. (1978). Sixty battered women. *Victimology,* 2(3-4), 460–70.

Holiman, M., and Schilit, R. (1991). Aftercare for battered women: How to encourage maintenance of change. *Psychotherapy,* 28, 345–53.

Homant, R.J., and Kennedy, D.B. (1985). Police perceptions of spouse abuse: A comparison of male and female officers. *Journal of Criminal Justice,* 13(1), 29–47.

Horowitz, M., Wilner, N, and Alvarez, W. (1979). Impact of Events Scale: A measure of subjective stress. *Psychosomatic Medicine,* 41(3), 209–18.

Hotaling, G., and Sugarman, D. (1990). A risk marker analysis of assaulted wives. *Journal of Family Violence,* 5(1), 1–13.

Houskamp, B., and Foy, D. (1991). The assessment of posttraumatic stress disorder in battered women. *Journal of Interpersonal Violence,* 6(3), 367–75.

Hudson, W. (1992). *WALMYR assessment scales scoring manual.* Tempe, AZ: WALMYR Publishing.

Hughes, H. (1988). Psychological and behavioral correlates of family violence in child witnesses and victims. *American Journal of Orthopsychiatry,* 58(1), 77–90.

Hughes, H., and Barad, S. (1983). Psychological functioning of children in a battered women's shelter: A preliminary investigation. *American Journal of Orthopsychiatry,* 53, 525–31.

Hughes, H., and Hampton, K. (1984). Relationships between the affective functioning of physically abused and non-abused children and their mothers in shelters for battered women. Paper presented at the Annual Meeting of the American Psychological Association, Toronto.

Hughes, H., and Luke, D. (1998). Heterogeneity in adjustment among children of battered women. In G. Holden, R. Geffner, and E.N. Jouriles (Eds.), *Children exposed to marital violence: Theory, research, and applied issues* (pp. 185–221). Washington, DC: American Psychological Association.

Hughes, M.J., and Jones, L. (2000). Women, domestic violence and Posttraumatic Stress Disorder. *Family Therapy,* 27(3), 125–39.

Humphreys, C. (1997). *Case planning issues where domestic violence occurs in the context of child protection: A report for Coventry Social Services Child Protection Unit.* http://www.coventry.gov.uk/social/child/dome/caseplan/index
_____. (1999). Avoidance and confrontation: Social work practice in relation to domestic violence and child abuse. *Child and Family Social Work,* 4, 77–87.

Hutchison, E. (1992). Child welfare as a woman's issue. *Families in Society: The Journal of Contemporary Human Services,* 73(2), 67–78.

Ibrahim, F., and Herr, E. (1987). Battered women: A developmental life-career counselling perspective. *Journal of Counselling and Development,* 65, 244–48.

Jackson, M., and Dilger, R. (1995). An empowering approach to women's domestic violence groups. *Australian Social Work,* 48(1), 51–59.

Jaffe, P., Reitzel, D., Hastings, E., and Austin, G. (1991). *Wife assault as a crime: The perspectives of victims and police officers on a charging policy in London, Ontario, from 1980–1990.* London, ON: London Family Court Clinic.

Jaffe, P., Wilson, S., Cameron, S., Zajc, R., and Wolfe, D. (1987). Are children who witness wife battering "in need of protection"? *Ontario Association of Children's Aid Societies,* 31(7), 3–7.

Jaffe, P., Wolfe, D., and Wilson, S.K. (1990). *Children of battered women.* Newbury Park, CA: Sage.

Johnson, H. (1995). Seriousness, type and frequency of violence against wives. In M. Valverde, L. MacLeod and K. Johnson (Eds.), *Wife assault and the Canadian criminal justice system.* Toronto: University of Toronto Press

_____. (1996). *Dangerous domains: Violence against women in Canada.* Toronto: Nelson Publishers.

Johnson, I., Crowley, J., and Sigler, R. (1992). Agency response to domestic violence: Services provided to battered women. In E. Viano (Ed.), *Intimate violence: Interdisciplinary perspectives* (pp. 191–202). Washington, DC: Hemisphere.

Johnson, M. (1995). Patriarchal terrorism and common couple violence: Two forms of violence against women. *Journal of Marriage and the Family,* 57, 283–94.

Kanuha, V. (1990). Compounding the triple jeopardy: Battering in lesbian of color relationships. *Women and Therapy,* 9, 169–84.

Kemp, A., Green, B., Hovanitz, C., and Rawlings, E. (1995). Incidence and correlates of posttraumatic stress disorder in battered women. *Journal of Interpersonal Violence,* 10(1), 43–55.

Kemp, A., Rawlings, E., and Green, B. (1991). Post-traumatic stress disorder (PTSD) in battered women: A shelter sample. *Journal of Traumatic Stress,* 4(1), 1991.

Kolbo, J. (1996). Risk and resilience among children exposed to family violence. *Violence and Victims,* 11, 113–28.

Krane, J. (1997). Least disruptive and intrusive course of action … for whom? Insights from feminist analysis of practice in cases of child sexual abuse. In J. Pulkingham and G. Ternowetsky (Eds.), *Child and family policies: Struggles, strategies and options* (pp.58–74). Halifax, NS: Fernwood Publishing.

Kurtz, D. (1996). Separation, divorce, and woman abuse. *Violence Against Women,* 2(1), 63–81.

Lamb, S. (1999). Constructing the victim: Popular images and lasting labels. In S. Lamb (Ed.), *New versions of victims: Feminists struggle with the concept* (pp. 108–38). New York: New York University Press.

LaRocque, E. (1995). Violence in Aboriginal communities. In M. Valverde, L. MacLeod, and K. Johnson (Eds.), *Wife assault and the Canadian criminal justice system* (pp. 104–22). Toronto: Centre of Criminology, University of Toronto.

Law Reform Commission of Canada (1975). Working paper No. 15: *Criminal procedure: Control of the process.* Ottawa: Information Canada.

Law Reform Commission of Nova Scotia.(1995). *From rhetoric to reality—Ending domestic violence in Nova Scotia—Final report.* Halifax, NS.

Lerman, L.G. (1981). *Prosecution for spouse abuse: Innovations in criminal justice response*. Washington, DC: Center for Women Policy Studies.

Levendosky, A., Lynch, S., and Graham-Bermann, S. (2000). Mothers' perceptions of the impact of woman abuse on their parenting. *Violence Against Women*, 6, 247–71.

Liss, M.B., and Stahly, G.B. (1993) Domestic violence and child custody. In M. Hansen and M. Harway (Eds.), *Battering and family therapy: A feminist perspective* (pp. 175–87). Newbury Park, CA: Sage.

Lorde, A. (1996). *Sister Outsider: Essays and speeches*. Freedom, CA: Crossing Press.

MacIntyre, E. (1993). The historical context of child welfare in Canada. In B. Wharf (Ed.), *Rethinking child welfare in Canada* (pp. 13–36). Toronto: Oxford University Press.

MacLeod, F. (1989). *Transition house: How to establish a refuge for battered women*. Ottawa, ON: National Clearinghouse on Family Violence, Health and Welfare Canada.

MacLeod, L. (1987). *Battered but not beaten: Preventing wife battering in Canada*. Ottawa, ON: Canadian Advisory Council on the Status of Women.

_____. (1989). *Wife battering and the web of hope: Progress, dilemmas and visions of prevention*. Ottawa, ON: National Clearinghouse on Family Violence, Health and Welfare Canada.

Magen, R. (1999). In the best interests of battered women: Reconceptualizing allegations of failure to protect. *Child Maltreatment*, 4, 127–35.

Mahoney, M. (1991). Legal images of battered women: Redefining the issue of separation. *Michigan Law Review*, 90, 1–94.

Marecek, J. (1999). Trauma talk in feminist clinical practice. In S. Lamb (Ed.), *New versions of victims: Feminists struggle with the concept* (pp. 158–82). New York: New York University Press.

Marshall, C., and Rossman, G.B. (1989). *Designing qualitative research*. Newbury Park, CA: Sage.

McDonald, P.L. (1989). Transition houses and the problem of family violence. In B. Pressman, G. Cameron, and M. Rothery (Eds.), *Intervening with assaulted women: Current research, theory and practice* (pp. 111–23). Hillsdale, NJ: Lawrence Erlbaum.

McDonald, P.L., Chisholm, W., Peressini, T., and Smillie, T. (1986). *A review of a second stage shelter for battered women and their children*. Ottawa: Health and Welfare Canada, Project #4558-32-2.

McEvoy, M., and Daniluk, J. (1995). Wounds to the soul: The experiences of Aboriginal women survivors of sexual abuse. *Canadian Psychology*, 36(3), 221–35.

McGillivray, A., and Comaskey, B. (1996). *Intimate violence, aboriginal women and justice system response: A Winnipeg study*. Winnipeg, MB: Original Women's Network.

Mechanic, M.B., Weaver, T.L., and Resick, P. (2000). Intimate partner violence and stalking behavior: Explorations of patterns and correlates in a sample of acutely battered women. *Violence and Victims*, 15(1), 55–72.

Miccio, K. (1995). In the name of mothers and children: Deconstructing the myth of the passive battered mother and the "protected child" in child neglect proceedings. *Albany Law Review*, 58, 1087–107.

Mickish, J., and Schoen, K. (1988). Domestic violence: Developing and maintaining an effective policy. *Prosecutor*, 21(3), 15–20.

Miller, D. (1987). Children's policy and women's policy: Congruence or conflict? *Social Work*, 32, 289–92.

Milner, J. (1993). A disappearing act: The differing career paths of fathers and mothers in child protection investigations. *Critical Social Policy*, 13, 48–63.

Monson, C.M., and Langhinrichsen-Rohling, J. (1998). Sexual and nonsexual marital aggression: Legal considerations, epidemiology, and an integrated typology of perpetrators. *Aggression and Violent Behavior*, 3(4), 369–89.

Moore, D. (Ed.). (1979). *Battered women*. Beverly Hills, CA: Sage.

Moore, T., Pepler, D., Mae, R., and Kates, M. (1989). Effects of family violence on children: New directions for research and intervention. In B. Pressman, G. Cameron, and M. Rothery (Eds.), *Intervening with assaulted women: Current theory, research, and practice* (pp. 75–91). Hillsdale, NJ.: Lawrence Erlbaum Associates.

Moore, T., Peplar, D., Weinberg, B., Hammond, L., Waddell, J., and Weiser, L. (1990). Research on children from violent families. *Canada's Mental Health*, 38(2/3), 19-22.

Mullender, A. (1996). *Rethinking domestic violence: The social work and probation response*. New York: Routledge.

National Council of Juvenile and Family Court Judges Family Violence Department. (1999). *Effective intervention in domestic violence and child maltreatment cases: Guidelines for policy and practice*. Reno, NV: National Council of Juvenile and Family Court Judges.

NiCarthy, G., Merriam, K., and Coffman, S. (1984). *Talking it out: A guide to groups for abused women*. Seattle, WA: Seal Press.

Okun, L. (1988). Termination or resumption of cohabitation in woman battering relationships: A statistical study. In G. Hotaling, D. Finkelhor, J. Kirkpatrick, and M. Straus (Ed.), *Coping with family violence: Research and policy perspectives* (pp. 107–19). Newbury Park, CA: Sage.

Orava, T.A., McLeod, P., and Sharpe, D. (1996). Perceptions of control, depressive symptomatology, and self-esteem of women in transition from abusive relationships. *Journal of Family Violence*, 11(2), 167–86.

Parkinson, P., and Humphreys, C. (1998). Children who witness domestic violence: The implications for child protection. *Child and Family Law Quarterly*, 10, 147–59.

Peled, E. (1993). Children who witness women battering: Concerns and dilemmas in the construction of a social problem. *Children and Youth Services Review*, 15, 43–52.

Peled, E., and Edleson, J. (1994). Advocacy for battered women: A national survey. *Journal of Family Violence*, 9(3), 285–96.

Pence, E., and Paymar, M. (1993). *Education groups for men who batter: The Duluth model*. New York: Springer.

Poels, Y., and Berger, J. (1992). Group work with survivors of domestic violence. *Australian Social Work*, 45(4), 41–47.

Pottie-Bunge, V., and Levett, A. (1998). *Family violence in Canada: A statistical profile*. Ottawa: Canadian Centre for Justice Statistics, Statistics Canada.

Pressman, B. (1984). *Family violence: Origins and treatment*. Guelph, ON: Office for Educational Practice. University of Guelph.

_____. (1989). Treatment of wife-abuse: The case for feminist therapy. In B.

Pressman, G. Cameron, and M. Rothery (Eds.), *Intervening with assaulted women: Current theory, research and practice* (pp. 21–45). Hillsdale, NJ: Lawrence Erlbaum Associates.

Prud'homme, D. (1994). Impact des maisons d'hérbergement sur les femmes violentées et leurs enfants. In M. Rinfret-Raynor and S. Cantin (Eds.), *Violence conjugale: Reserches sur la violence faite aux femmes en milieu conjugal*. Montreal: Gaetan Morin.

Razack, S. (1998). *Looking white people in the eye*. Toronto: University of Toronto Press.

Renzetti, C.M. (1992). *Violent betrayal: Partner abuse in lesbian relationships*. Newbury Park, CA: Sage.

_____. (1998). Violence and abuse in lesbian relationships: Theoretical and empirical issues. In R.K. Bergen (Ed.), *Issues in intimate violence* (pp. 117–28). Thousand Oak, CA: Sage.

Rhodes, N.R., and McKenzie, Baranoff E. (1998). Why do battered women stay? Three decades of research. *Aggression and Violent Behavior*, 3(4), 391–406.

Rigakos, G.S., and Bonneycastle, K.D. (Eds.). (1998). *Unsettling truths: Battered women, policy, politics, and contemporary Canadian research*, Vancouver, BC: Vancouver Collective Press.

Riggs, D.S., Kilpatrick, D.G., and Resnick, H. (1992). Long-term psychological distress associated with marital rape and aggravated assault: A comparison to other crime victims. *Journal of Family Violence*, 7(4), 283–96.

Rinfret-Raynor, M., and Cantin, S. (1997). Feminist therapy for battered women: An assessment. In G. Kaufman Kantor and J.L. Jasinski (Eds.), *Out of the darkness: Contemporary perspectives on family violence* (pp.219–34). Thousand Oaks, CA: Sage.

Rinfret-Raynor, M., Paquet-Deehy, A., Larouche, G., and Cantin, S. (1992). *Intervening with battered women: Evaluating the effectiveness of a feminist model*. Ottawa, ON: National Clearinghouse of Family Violence, Health and Welfare Canada.

Ristock, J.L. (1995). *The impact of violence in mental health: A guide to the literature*. Ottawa, ON: Health Canada.

_____. (1997). The cultural politics of abuse in lesbian relationships: Challenges for community action. In N. Benokraitis (Ed.), *Subtle sexism: Current practice and prospects for change* (pp. 279–96). Thousand Oaks, CA: Sage.

_____. (1998). Community-based research: Lesbian abuse and other telling tales. In J.L. Ristock and C.G. Taylor (Eds.), *Inside the academy and out: Lesbian/gay/queer studies and social action* (pp. 137–54). Toronto: University of Toronto Press.

_____. (in press). Exploring dynamics of abusive lesbian relationships: Preliminary analysis of a multi-site, qualitative study. *American Journal of Community Psychology*.

Ristock, J.L., and Pennell, J. (1996). *Community research as empowerment: Feminist links, postmodern interruptions*. Toronto: Oxford University Press.

Roberts, A.R. (1998). *Battered women and their families: Intervention strategies and treatment approaches (2nd ed.)*. New York: Springer.

Rodgers, K. (1994). Wife assault: The findings of a national survey. *Juristat*

Service Bulletin: Canadian Centre for Justice Statistics, 14(9), 1–21. Ottawa, ON: Minister of Industry, Science and Technology.

Rosenbaum, A., and O'Leary, K. (1981). Children: The unintended victims of marital violence. *American Journal of Orthopsychiatry,* 51, 692–99.

Rothery, M.A., Tutty, L.M., and Grinnell, R.M. Jr. (1996). Phase one: Planning your study. In L.M. Tutty, M.A. Rothery, and R.M. Grinnell Jr. (Eds.), *Qualitative research for social workers* (pp. 24–49). Toronto: Allyn and Bacon.

Rothery, M., Tutty, L., and Weaver, G. (1999). Touch choices: Women, abusive partners and the ecology of decision-making. *Canadian Journal of Community Mental Health,* 18(1) 5–18.

Rubin, A. (1991). The effectiveness of outreach counseling and support groups for battered women: A preliminary evaluation. *Research on Social Work Practice,* 1, 332–57.

Rubin, H., and Rubin, I. (1995). *Qualitative interviewing: The art of hearing data.* Thousand Oaks, CA: Sage.

Russell, M. (1990). Second stage shelters: A consumer's report. *Canada's Mental Health,* 38(2/3), 24–27.

Russell, M., Forcier, C., and Charles, M. (1987). *Safe Choice: Client satisfaction survey.* Report prepared for Act II, Vancouver, British Columbia.

Sackett, L.A., and Saunders, D.G. (1999). The impact of different forms of psychological abuse on battered women. *Violence and Victims,* 14(1), 105–17.

Sakai, C. (1991). Group intervention strategies with domestic abusers. *Families in Society: The Journal of Contemporary Human Services,* 72(9), 536–42.

Saunders, D.G. (1994). Posttraumatic stress symptom profiles of battered women: A comparison of survivors in two settings. *Violence and Victims,* 9(1), 31–44.

Savage, S. (1987). *Group treatment for abusive men and their partners,* London, ON: Family Service London.

Schechter, S., and Edleson, J. (1995). In the best interest of women and children: A call for collaboration between child welfare and domestic violence constituencies. *Protecting Children,* 11, 6–11.

Scherzer, T. (1998). Domestic violence in lesbian relationships: Findings of the lesbian relationships research project. *Journal of Lesbian Studies,* 2(1) 29–47.

Schmid, J.D., and Sherman, L.W. (1993). Does arrest deter domestic violence? *American Behavioural Scientist,* 36, 601–609.

Schmidt, J., and Steury, E.H. (1989). Prosecutorial discretion in filing charges in domestic violence cases. *Criminology,* 27, 487–510.

Schutte, N., Bouleige, L., and Malouf, J. (1986). Returning to a partner after leaving a crisis shelter: A decision faced by battered women. *Journal of Social Behavior and Personality,* 1(2), 295–98.

Self-Help Canada Series. (1993). *Peer-facilitated support groups for abused women* (Cat. H72-21-90-1993). Ottawa, ON: National Clearinghouse on Family Violence, Health and Welfare Canada.

Smillie, T. (1991). *Why women return to battering relationships.* Unpublished M.S.W. project. University of Calgary.

Snider, L. (1998). Struggles for justice: Criminalization and alternatives" In K. Bonneycastle and G. Rigakos, (Eds.), *Unsettling truths: Battered women, policy, politics, and contemporary Canadian research* (pp. 144–55). Vancouver,

BC: Collective Press.

Snyder, D., and Scheer, N. (1981). Predicting disposition following brief residence at a shelter for battered women. *American Journal of Community Psychology* 9(5),559–66.

Solomon, P.H. (1983). *Criminal justice policy: From research to reform.* Toronto: Butterworth.

SPR Associates (1997). A place to go: An evaluation of the Next Step program for second-stage housing in Canada. Ottawa, ON: Canada Mortgage and Housing Corporation.

Stanko, E. (1981–82). The impact of victim assessment on prosecutor's screening decisions: The case of the New York District Attorney's office. *Law and Society Review,* 16(2), 225–39.

Stanley, N. (1997). Domestic violence and child abuse: Developing social work practice. *Child and Family Social Work,* 2, 135–45.

Stark, E. (1984). *The battering syndrome: Social knowledge, social therapy and the abuse of women.* Ann Arbor, MI: University Microfilms International.

_____. (1993). Mandatory arrest of batterers: A reply to its critics. *American Behavioral Scientist,* 36 (5), 651–80.

Statistics Canada (2000). *Family violence in Canada: A statistical profile 2000.* Ottawa, ON.

_____. (1999/2000). *Transition home survey.* Ottawa, ON.

Statutes of Alberta (1997). *Child Welfare Act (Volume 3).* Edmonton, Alberta.

Statutes of Manitoba (1999). *Domestic Violence and Stalking, Protection, Prevention and Compensation Act (Volume 41).* Winnipeg, Manitoba.

Statutes of Saskatchewan (1994). *Victims of Violence Act (Volume 6.02).* Regina, Saskatchewan.

_____. (1994.) *Victims of Domestic Violence Assistance Act (Volume 6.2).* Regina Saskatchewan.

Stephens, N., McDonald, R., and Jouriles, E. (2000). Helping children who reside at shelters for battered women: Lessons learned. In R. Geffner, P. Jaffe, and M. Sudermann, (Eds.), *Children exposed to domestic violence: Current issues in research, intervention, prevention, and policy development* (pp. 147–60). New York: The Haworth Press.

Stout, K.D., and McPhail, B. (1998). *Confronting sexism and violence against women.* New York: Longman.

Strange, C. (1995). Historical perspective of wife assault. In M. Valverde, L., MacLeod, and K. Johnson, (Eds.), *Wife assault and the Canadian Criminal Justice System* (pp. 293–304). Toronto: Centre of Criminology, University of Toronto.

Straus, M. (1990). Injury and frequency of assault and the "Representative sample fallacy" in measuring wife beating and child abuse. In M. Straus and R. Gelles (Eds.), *Physical violence in American families* (pp. 75–94). New Brunswick, NJ: Transaction Press.

Straus, M., and Gelles, R. (1996). *Physical violence in American families.* New Brunswick, NJ: Transaction Publishers.

Straus, M., Gelles, R., and Steinmetz, S. (1980). *Behind closed doors: Violence in the American family.* New York: Anchor Books.

Sudermann, M. (December, 1997). "Presentation to Panel of Experts on Child Protection." Unpublished paper.

Sullivan, C. (1991). The provision of advocacy services to women leaving abusive partners: An exploratory study. *Journal of Interpersonal Violence,* 6(1), 41–54.

Sullivan, C.M., Basta, J., Tan, C. and Davidson II, W.S. (1992). After the crisis: A needs assessment of women leaving a domestic violence shelter. *Violence and Victims,* 7(3), 267–75.

Sullivan, C., and Bybee, D.I. (1999). Reducing violence using community-based advocacy for women with abusive partners. *Journal of Consulting and Clinical Psychology,* 67(1), 43–53.

Sullivan, C., Campbell, R., Angelique, H., Eby, K., and Davidson II, W. (1994). An advocacy program for women with abusive partners: Six month follow-up. *American Journal of Community Psychology,* 22(1), 101–22.

Sullivan, C., and Davidson II, W. (1991). The provision of advocacy services to women leaving abusive partners: An examination of short-term effects. *American Journal of Community Psychology,* 19(6), 953–60.

Sullivan, C., Nguyen, H., Allen, N., Bybee, D., and Juras, J. (2000). Beyond searching for deficits: Evidence that physically and emotionally abused women are nurturing parents. *Journal of Emotional Abuse,* 2, 51–71.

Sullivan, C., Tan, C., Basta, J., Rumptz, M., and Davidson II, W. (1992). An advocacy intervention program for women with abusive partners: Initial evaluation. *American Journal of Community Psychology,* 20(3), 309–32.

Swift, K. (1998). Contradictions in child welfare: Neglect and responsibility. In C. Baines, P. Evans, and S. Neysmith (Eds.), *Women's caring: Feminist perspectives on social welfare* (pp. 160–87). Toronto: Oxford University Press.

Szinovacz, M.E., and Egley, L.C. (1995). Comparing one-partner and couple data on sensitive marital behaviors: The case of marital violence. *Journal of Marriage and the Family,* 57, 995–1010.

Tan, C., Basta, J., Sullivan, C.M., and Davidson II, W. (1995). The role of social support in the lives of women exiting domestic violence shelters: An experimental study. *Journal of Interpersonal Violence,* 10, 437–51.

Trimpey, M. (1989). Self esteem and anxiety: Key issues in an abused women's support group. *Issues in Mental Health Nursing,* 10, 297–308.

Tutty, L. (1993). After the shelter: Critical issues for women who leave assaultive relationships. *Canadian Social Work Review,* 10(2), 183–201.

_____. (1996). Post shelter services: The efficacy of follow-up programs for abused women. *Research on Social Work Practice,* 6(4), 425–41.

_____. (1998). Mental health issues of abused women: The perceptions of shelter workers. *Canadian Journal of Community Mental Health,* 17(1), 79–102.

_____. (1999a). *Husband abuse: An overview of research and perspectives.* Ottawa, ON: National Clearinghouse on Family Violence, Health and Welfare Canada.

_____. (1999b). Considering emotional abuse in the link between spouse and child abuse. *Journal of Emotional Abuse,* 1(4) 53–79.

_____. (in press). *Shelters for abused women in Canada: A celebration of the past, challenges for the future.* Ottawa, ON: Family Violence Prevention, Health Canada.

Tutty, L., Bidgood, B., and Rothery, M. (1993). Support groups for battered women: Research on their efficacy. *Journal of Family Violence,* 8(4), 325-1-19.

_____. (1996). The impact of group process and client variables in support groups for battered women. *Research on Social Work Practice*, 6(3), 308–24.

Tutty, L., and Rothery, M. (June, 1997). Women who seek shelter from wife assault: Risk assessment and service needs. Paper presented at the 5th International Family Violence Research Conference, Durham, New Hampshire.

_____. (1997). *What went right: Working relationships in Alberta shelters for abused women*. Edmonton, AB: Alberta Council of Women's Shelters.

_____. (1999, July). What happens to high-risk women after shelter residence? 6th International Family Violence Research Conference, University of New Hampshire, Durham, NH.

_____. (in press). Beyond shelters: Support groups and community-based advocacy for abused women. In A.R. Roberts (Ed.), *Helping battered women: New perspectives and remedies (second edition)*. New York: Oxford University Press.

Tutty, L., Rothery, M., Cox, G., and Richardson, C. (1995). *An evaluation of the Calgary YWCA family violence programs: Assisting battered women and their children*. Final Report to the Family Violence Prevention Division, Health Canada.

Tutty, L., and Wagar, J. (1994). The evolution of a group for young children who have witnessed family violence. *Social Work With Groups*, 17(1/2), 89–104.

Tutty, L.M., Weaver, G., and Rothery, M.A. (1999). Resident's views of the efficacy of shelter services for abused women. *Violence Against Women*, 5(8), 869–925.

Ursel, J. (1992). A progress report on the Family Violence Court in Winnipeg. *Manitoba Law Journal*, 21, 100–30.

_____. (1995). The Winnipeg Family Violence Court. In M. Valverde, L., MacLeod and K. Johnson (Eds.),*Wife assault and the Canadian criminal justice system*. Toronto: University of Toronto Press, Toronto.

_____. (1998). Mandatory charging: The Manitoba model. In G.S. Rigakos and K.D. Bonneycastle (Eds.), *Unsettling truths: Battered women, policy, politics, and contemporary Canadian research* (pp. 73–81). Vancouver, BC: Collective Press.

_____. (2001). *Report on domestic violence polices and their impact on Aboriginal people*. Submitted to the Aboriginal Justice Implementation Commission, February. [on-line at: http://www.ajic.mb.ca/consult.html]

Verdun-Jones, S.N., and Hatch, A.J. (1985). *Plea bargaining and sentencing in Canada*. Ottawa, ON: The Canadian Sentencing Commission.

Vitanza, S., Vogel, L., and Marshall, L. (1995). Distress and symptoms of post-traumatic stress disorder in abused women. *Violence and Victims*, 10(1), 23–34.

Waldron, C. (1996). Lesbians of colour and the domestic violence movement. In C. Renzetti and C. Miley (Eds.), *Violence in gay and lesbian domestic partnerships* (pp. 43–51). New York: Harrington Park Press.

Walker, G. (1990). *Family violence and the women's movement: The conceptual politics of struggle*. Toronto: University of Toronto Press.

Walker, L. (1978). Battered women and learned helplessness. *Victimology*, 2(3-4), 525–34.

_____. (1984). *The battered women syndrome*. New York: Springer.

_____. (1991). Post-traumatic stress disorder in women: Diagnosis and treatment of battered woman syndrome. *Psychotherapy*, 28(1), 21–29.

Weisz, G., Taggart, J., Mockler, S., and Streich, P. (1994). *The role of housing in dealing with family violence in Canada*. Ottawa, ON: Canada Mortgage and Housing Corporation.

Wetzel, L., and Ross, M. (1983). Psychological and social ramifications of battering: Observations leading to a counselling methodology for victims of domestic violence. *Personnel and Guidance Journal*, 61(7), 423–28.

Whalen, M. (1996). *Counselling to end violence against women: A subversive model*. Thousand Oaks, CA: Sage.

Wharf, B., and McKenzie, B. (1998). *Connecting policy to practice in the human services*. Toronto: Oxford University Press.

Whatley, M.A. (1993). For better or worse: The case of marital rape. *Violence and Victims*, 8(1), 29–39).

Whitney, P., and Davis, L. (1999). Child abuse and domestic violence in Massachusetts: Can practice be integrated in a public child welfare setting? *Child Maltreatment*, 4, 158–66.

Wilson, K., Vercella, R., Brems, C., Benning, D., and Renfro, N. (1992). Levels of learned helplessness in abused women. *Women and Therapy*, 13(4), 53–67.

Wilson, M., Baglioni, A., and Downing, D. (1989). Analysing factors influencing readmission to a battered woman's shelter. *Journal of Family Violence*, 4(3), 275–84.

Wilson, M.I., and Daly, M. (1992). Who kills whom in spousal killings? On the exceptional sex ratio of spousal homicides in the United States. *Criminology*, 30(2), 189–213.

Wood, G.G., and Middleman, R.R. (1992). Groups to empower battered women. *Affilia*, 3, 62–68.

Worden, A.P. (2000). The changing boundaries of the criminal justice system: Redefining the problem and the response in domestic violence. *Criminal Justice 2000* (pp. 215–66). Washington, DC: U.S. Department of Justice. www.ojp.usdoj.gov/nij/criminal_justice2000/vol2_200.html

Wright, J.A., Burgess, A.G., Laszlo, A.T., McCrary, G.O., and Douglas, J.E. (1996). A typology of interpersonal stalking. *Journal of Interpersonal Violence*, 11(4), 487–502.

Yalom, I.D. (1975). *The theory and practice of group psychotherapy*. New York: Basic Books.

Yllo, K. (1993). Through a feminist lens: Gender, power and violence. In R. Gelles and D. Loseke (Eds.), *Current controversies on family violence* (pp. 47–62.). Newbury Park, CA: Sage.